EISENHOWER'S
SIX GREAT DECISIONS

GENERAL WALTER BEDELL SMITH

Former Chief of Staff of the Allied Expeditionary Force in Europe

★★

EISENHOWER'S

Six Great Decisions

[EUROPE 1944-1945]

★★

LONGMANS, GREEN AND CO.

NEW YORK ★ LONDON ★ TORONTO

1956

LONGMANS, GREEN AND CO., INC.
55 FIFTH AVENUE, NEW YORK 3

LONGMANS, GREEN AND CO., LTD.
6 & 7 CLIFFORD STREET, LONDON W 1

LONGMANS, GREEN AND CO.
20 CRANFIELD ROAD, TORONTO 16

Acknowledgment

The idea of this narrative originated with my friend
Mr. Demaree Bess, Associate Editor of the *Saturday
Evening Post*, which first published much of it. Mr. Bess
knew of the careful daily records maintained by the
General Shaff Secretariat of SHAEF, and he felt that an
early postwar account should be written of the several
decisions which I have described as vital to our success
in the West.

I was reluctant to undertake the task during the short
period within which I was turning over my recently
assumed duties with the War Department General Staff
prior to proceeding to Moscow and would not have
done so except for two important considerations. The
first of these was that Sir Winston Churchill, then visiting in the United States, urged me to do it. He felt that
accounts would be written by participants of both nationalities from a less impartial viewpoint, and that as
a result there might, during the critical postwar years,
be some loss of that feeling of common purpose and

ability to work together which we developed during the period of crisis and hazard.

The second was the willingness of Colonel Stewart Beach, formerly of the War Department General Staff and now Executive Editor of *This Week* magazine, to put my rambling dictation into understandable sequence. I am greatly indebted to him for this, and for preparing, from even more meager notes, the first draft of the added and previously unpublished chapters.

Colonels Daniel Gilmore, J. B. Moore, and Carter Burgess (now Assistant Secretary of Defense), who were successively secretaries of the General Staff of Supreme Headquarters, were responsible for the remarkably accurate and complete daily records from which this account is condensed.

—Walter Bedell Smith
General, U.S.A. (Ret.)

Contents

Maps

Maps

EISENHOWER'S
SIX GREAT DECISIONS

Prelude to Invasion

THE chapters which follow tell the story of six crucial decisions by General Eisenhower, Supreme Commander of the Allied Expeditionary Force. As I viewed them then, and as I review them now, these were the major decisions which carried us to overwhelming victory in Europe eleven months from the June dawn when our mighty armada assaulted the beaches of Normandy. Each presented the alternatives of success or failure, victory or defeat, and in this respect they differ from the many important decisions which must be made daily by a high commander. For this reason, each episode is related as a single narrative, complete in itself. But together they are the high points in the progress of our forces across Europe. They sketch the design by which we played our part in destroying the ability of Hitler to make war.

The accounts of what happened were written a few months after the German surrender. They were distilled from very complete staff papers, from the records of in-

1

numerable conferences, and from the fresh reservoir of
my memory. They are often rounded out by statements
of enemy commanders, captured during the course of
hostilities. These tell the German side and reveal why
the Nazis reacted as they did. But because these great
events took place more than a decade ago, I think some
background is necessary to give them perspective. It
properly begins on September 7, 1942, when I first reported to General Eisenhower in England.

Since the previous June he had been serving in London as Commanding General, European Theater of
Operations, United States Army, which at that time
comprised only the United Kingdom and Iceland. At
the beginning I was to act as his Chief of Staff at this
headquarters. But the decision to invade North Africa
was confirmed on July 26, and since that time planning
for this operation, code-named TORCH, had been proceeding under General Eisenhower's direction. He was
now not only the Theater Commander but had been
designated in mid-August as Commander in Chief of
the Allied Expeditionary Forces for the Mediterranean
campaign. After familiarizing myself with details and
routines at theater headquarters, I also assumed the duties
of Chief of Staff at the Allied headquarters, where a staff
of American and British officers was planning the first
great combined offensive against the Axis war machine.

The North African campaign furnished invaluable experience in the operation of an Allied staff. The two
nationalities had to learn to live together, then to work
together. There was some friction at first, but it was

soon rubbed off with the realization of General Eisenhower's determination that his staff would be Allied in every respect. The individual's professional ability was what counted, not his uniform. When I went back to England as OVERLORD's Chief of Staff, the officers who had served in an Allied headquarters fitted smoothly into SHAEF. Newcomers had some difficulty, but they soon caught the spirit. If they failed to do so, they were relieved, regardless of nationality.

One of our first minor problems in North Africa had to be agreement on a common military language. It was surprising both to British and Americans to find that usage differed sharply on words for quite common things. I remember one occasion in Algiers when, in looking over a list of railway supply requirements, General Eisenhower questioned what seemed to be an astronomical number of "sleepers." But the English word "sleeper" has its American equivalent in "tie"—the ties on which railroad tracks are laid. These differences in language are often amusing, but in a military operation they can be serious by reason of the confusion of purpose they might cause. We quickly established a common vocabulary, using some English and some American expressions. After a short time we used them so instinctively that their origin was forgotten.

The months of battle which carried us to our Tunisian victory in May, 1943, and the subsequent Sicilian and Italian campaigns, form no proper part of the present account. During this period, however, a staff of American and British planners, under the direction of Lt. Gen.

Sir Frederick E. Morgan, was at work in London drawing up preliminary plans for the proposed assault on northwest Europe. This headquarters was known as COSSAC, from General Morgan's title—Chief of Staff to the Supreme Allied Commander (designate). In July, 1943, they presented their blueprint to the Combined Chiefs of Staff, and full approval of the operation was given at the Quebec Conference in August, 1943. The target date was set for May 1, 1944.

As yet, no commander had been named for the Allied force, but the operation was taking shape rapidly. In early September General Omar N. Bradley was detached from command of II Corps in Sicily and designated commander of the United States First Army, to be composed of American troops who would take part in the Normandy landings. I met General Bradley at our advanced Sicilian command post near Catania in the shadow of Mt. Etna on the morning General Eisenhower informed him of his good fortune. Bradley flew to England almost immediately to take up his new duties. But back in the Mediterranean theater we remained deep in the problems and difficulties of the frustrating campaign up the Italian boot. It was early December before the choice of a Supreme Commander was finally made by the heads of state.

The decision was reached when President Roosevelt and Prime Minister Churchill met at the Cairo Conference. First word of it came to Algiers early on the morning of December 7, by pure coincidence the second anniversary of the attack on Pearl Harbor, in a message sent by General Marshall to General Eisenhower from Cairo. This message also indicated that I was to remain in the Mediterranean as both Chief of Staff of the new Allied Commander in Chief and Theater Commander for the American forces. I have never questioned a military assignment, but this was a great disappointment, in spite of the implied promotion, and I was naturally pleased when General Eisenhower informed me that he would insist on taking me with him to London as Chief of Staff for OVERLORD, the code name which had been selected as early as the spring of 1942 for the cross-Channel invasion. Our new assignments would begin in January.

We had little time to discuss plans that day. The President and his party arrived from Cairo by C-54 that afternoon. The following day, with the President, General Eisenhower, and the presidential party, I flew to Malta where Mr. Roosevelt presented a testimonial from America to Malta's bravery during the pounding this island bastion had taken from Axis bombers. Just previous to the Malta landing, hydraulic pressure failed in the mechanism responsible for lowering the wing flaps of the C-54. We were delayed on the island for two hours while repairs were made and then went on to Sicily where the President reviewed American troops and presented decorations to General Clark, for his bravery and leadership in the Salerno campaign, and half a dozen other officers. Without my knowledge I had been included on this list but I had taken the opportunity to confer with members of the staff elsewhere and could not be found when the ceremony took place. The President gave me the medal later, with somewhat less ceremony.

The presidential party returned to Tunis for the night and early the following morning took off for the flight back to Washington by way of Dakar. During the brief and crowded visit, General Eisenhower had several opportunities to talk with the President, who told him personally of his appointment to command OVERLORD. As yet, no title had been decided on for the Commander, though it had perhaps been foreshadowed in the naming of COSSAC. In the North African operation, General Eisenhower's title was Commander in Chief, Allied Expeditionary Forces. But it was not until Christmas Eve, 1943, that President Roosevelt announced in the course of a radio fireside talk that General Eisenhower was to be Supreme Commander, Allied Expeditionary Force, when we struck at Fortress Europa. It followed that the designation of his headquarters would be Supreme Headquarters, Allied Expeditionary Force, and from the initials of these words the accepted abbreviation of SHAEF came into existence.

General Eisenhower flew to the United States on New Year's Day, 1944, for conferences with General Marshall in Washington. Shortly after I left by plane for London. There I went immediately to Norfolk House, in St. James's Square, where the COSSAC planners were installed. This was the staff I would take over from General Morgan as the nucleus of the staff for SHAEF. Morgan, whom I considered indispensable, generously agreed to remain as deputy, although he might have had command of a corps.

For those who are unfamiliar with the military establishment, I think it may be useful to give a brief summary of the purpose and duties of the staff which functions for a high commander in war under the general direction of a chief of staff. Its broad mission is to draw up strategic plans, provide information on the disposition and capabilities of the enemy forces, allocate the troop units to the operation, and estimate the supplies necessary to bring the commander victory in the field. It is the duty of the staff to anticipate all foreseeable problems which the armies may meet and to recommend solutions. Its ultimate purpose is to free the commander from countless details of administration and organization and thus leave his mind clear to consider only the great purpose which he has been designated to carry out and to make the major decisions which he alone can make.

The general staff is divided functionally into several sections, each headed by a general officer who has the title of Assistant Chief of Staff, followed by the designation of his section. The four basic sections are abbreviated G-1, G-2, G-3, and G-4 (there may be others). The first of these, G-1, deals with personnel. It formulates the policies which govern the handling of the soldier as an individual, including, among other things, his morale and general welfare, his assignment, and his replacement if incapacitated.

G-2 is Intelligence. It collects and evaluates from many sources every obtainable scrap of information about the enemy. It seeks to learn where his forces are located, the extent of his defenses at every point of the territory he holds. It traces the movements of enemy divisions in and out of the line and evaluates from this and other information what these shifts may mean. When our troops began moving across the Channel on D-Day, the location of every German division in northwest France was pinpointed on the tactical commanders' battle maps. In our war room at SHAEF we had marked in the disposition of every enemy unit in all Europe. From this information we could immediately trace the movement of reinforcements to the battle area. It is an interesting fact that during the critical fighting in Normandy only one German division arrived on our front as a surprise.

Just ten days before the invasion, Intelligence brought news that three German divisions had been moved to the base of the Cotentin Peninsula, almost at the spot where our 82nd Airborne Division was scheduled to drop. As a result, the drop zone was moved nearer Utah Beach and north of the zone of the 101st Airborne. The 82nd was given the mission of seizing the roadhead at Ste Mère Eglise to protect the beach against a possible counterattack by enemy troops on the Cotentin Peninsula. On June 5, just after General Bradley had gone aboard Admiral Kirk's flagship *Augusta* for the invasion, we were able to get word to one of his officers still in Plymouth that the excellent German 352nd Infantry Division had moved to the area of Omaha Beach. It was too late for General Bradley to warn the assault troops, since radio silence had to be observed throughout the invasion fleet. And, before it was cut to pieces, the 352nd gave all too good an account of itself against the American 1st and 29th divisions the following day.

The G-3 section of the staff is concerned with preparation of the battle plans and the assignment of the major units which are to carry them out. Working from a directive which states the objectives to be gained, it is the mission of the Assistant Chief of Staff, G-3, to develop the tactics and to make assignments of units from the troops available. His plans must always depend on the supplies of every nature which the troops will require in the field.

G-4 deals with supply and transport. For such an enormous undertaking as Operation OVERLORD the extent and intricacy of this phase of the planning were almost beyond belief. Everything that a soldier requires for success in battle must be furnished to him. There must be food to feed him, ammunition for the weapon he uses, medical supplies if he is wounded, transport to carry him to the point of contact with the enemy. And transport means gasoline—thousands and hundreds of thousands of gallons once troops are on the move. To meet this need, our Engineers planned to lay pipelines on the Channel floor, and the first of these, stretching seventy miles from Sandown Bay on the Isle of Wight to Nacqueville, went into operation on August 12, before we broke out of the lodgement area in Normandy.

For such an amphibious operation as OVERLORD, all the vessels which carry troops and supplies are "combat-loaded," another problem which calls for the most minute planning on the part of G-4. The technique had been developed for the North African operation when ships were combat-loaded in both Great Britain and the United States for the assault. The purpose is to establish the priority of weapons, supplies, and transport as the troops will need them from the moment they are set down on a hostile shore. This priority is then followed on the vessels transporting each unit of troops so that the required matériel will be ready to hand when it is called for. The rule is that what will be needed first is last to be loaded on the ship. And while the routine seems simple, each officer who takes part in the invasion feels that his own effort requires a priority over some other need.

How complex these needs can be is indicated by some of the priorities assigned to the American First Army which was to strike Omaha and Utah beaches in the D-Day dawn. Something over fifty-five thousand American troops were to land on the beaches that day. The basic needs were easy enough to write down—food, ammunition, transport. But in addition there were 120-foot steel span bridges which Intelligence had pointed out would be necessary to carry transport over rivers and flooded areas. There were sulpha pills. If a bulldozer, needed immediately at one of the beaches, was not available when required, lives and time would be lost. There was fresh drinking water—more than three hundred thousand gallons for the first three days ashore. Everything had to be anticipated by G-4, and the staff at SHAEF had to check all these plans, confirm them, and ask the Supreme Commander to approve them, too. Supporting and working with the general staff is the special staff, groups of technical experts each headed, as in the case of the general staff, by a senior officer whose title is descriptive of his fuction. The Surgeon General, the Chief of Engineers, the Quartermaster General, and the Chief of Ordnance are examples among others. At the headquarters of a theater of operations the special staff is, relatively, quite large since its various sections must cover all of the activities and responsibilities of the theater.

At Supreme Headquarters the personnel of the three arms, Army, Navy, and Air, were integrated for all practical purposes and they lived and worked together.

Most of the detailed plans were not made at SHAEF itself. Reporting to the staff at Supreme Headquarters were the subordinate staffs of the commanders of the three combat arms—air, ground, and sea. These staffs carried on the tactical planning for the assault, the gaining of a bridgehead, and the build-up in the lodgement area which would precede our break-through onto the plains of Normandy. General Eisenhower himself would take over tactical command of the ground forces once we were established on the Continent. In the preliminary phases command was held by Field Marshal Sir Bernard L. Montgomery as commander of the 21st Army Group. General Bradley's American First Army was part of this force during the invasion. His headquarters was at Bristol, where his staff prepared the plans for pressing the war at the western end of the invasion line and taking the port of Cherbourg. But because General Bradley was also to command an American army group after the break-through, separated from Montgomery and reporting directly to General Eisenhower as over-all tactical commander, he had established a separate headquarters and staff for this higher command which reported to SHAEF. The American First Army, for the time being, was under command of Field Marshal Montgomery, but the American 12th Army Group was always to be separate from Montgomery's 21st Army Group.

Once more I feel I must digress briefly for those who are not familiar with military terms to discuss the chain of command in Operation OVERLORD and to explain some of the terms involved. As Supreme Commander, General Eisenhower was in direct command of the forces dedicated to the conquest of Hitler's armies. Under him was a deputy supreme commander, Air Chief Marshal Sir Arthur W. Tedder. The Supreme Headquarters staff reported to them. In the next echelon stood the Commander in Chief, Allied Naval Forces, the United States Army Group Commander (General Bradley), the British Army Group Commander (Field Marshal Montgomery), and the Commander in Chief, Allied Expeditionary Air Forces. Arrayed below these headquarters were the British and American naval and air commanders.

If the terms here are somewhat technical, let me start with a division which, in World War II, comprised about seventeen thousand men. The next higher echelon is a corps, composed of two or more divisions and various corps troops. For the invasion of Normandy, the Americans employed two corps, composed of two divisions each. The British also employed two corps, comprising both British and Canadian troops. Next above corps headquarters there is the army, composed of two or more corps. General Bradley's First Army, originally comprised of four divisions for the assault, had re-established command over all the other divisions which came across the Normandy beaches of his American area during the build-up.

The responsibility of a staff chief and his principal assistants is to direct planning, coordinate the planning of subordinate headquarters, and to make such decisions as are possible without the personal intervention of the Supreme Commander. Such decisions are made in his name and by his delegated authority. Where really important decisions were involved, the problems had to be presented to General Eisenhower. He made literally thousands of decisions in the days between January and June which need not concern us here. Since this narrative deals with his six crucial decisions, I think it should be established just how utterly the military system makes this matter of decision the responsibility of one man— the commander. Only thus can be made clear the awful responsibility which one man accepts when he occupies the position of supreme commander in a major theater of war, where the victory is to be achieved.

In the military system, the chain of command is absolute. Each commander in that chain is responsible as an

individual for his own decisions. In turn, he is responsible
to the next higher commander. General Eisenhower, as
Supreme Commander of the Allied Expeditionary Force,
was responsible for each decision his subordinates made.
This, in turn, indicates how carefully the high commander must weigh the choice of his division, corps, and
army commanders, since, if a subordinate commander
fails, it is the Supreme Commander who is at fault for
having placed him in a position of command.

During a D-Day broadcast, Major George Fielding
Eliot said, ". . . the present American Army is the most
capably commanded army which the United States has
ever placed in the field at the outset of a war. . . . Every
American general who now commands a division, a
corps or an army of American troops, has now been put
through this hard and unforgiving mill of trial. Those
who have failed in any degree have been relegated to
noncombat duties or to the retired list."

The same could have been said of our British con-
tingent, with even more force because of their years of
trial by combat.

General Eisenhower's "commander" was the Combined Chiefs of Staff whose headquarters was in Washington. I was intimately familiar with the functioning of
this command group since I was appointed its first
American secretary when it was brought into being in
Washington shortly after the Pearl Harbor attack. The
Combined Chiefs of Staff exercised over-all command
of British and American operations in all theaters of war.
They, in turn, were responsible only to the heads of

government—to President Roosevelt in the United States, to Prime Minister Churchill in the United Kingdom.

General Eisenhower's directive to command OVER-LORD was issued by the Combined Chiefs of Staff. Though the appointment had been made in December, 1943, it was on Lincoln's Birthday, February 12, 1944, that the directive was issued. I think it is important to quote this, since a directive establishes the broad latitude given to a commander within which he is authorized to establish his own policies. The directive fixes responsibility on the individual commander. It is left to him to decide how it is to be carried out. Here is General Eisenhower's directive:

1. You are hereby designated as Supreme Allied Commander of the forces planned under your orders for operations for liberation of Europe from Germans. Your title will be Supreme Commander Allied Expeditionary Force.

2. *Task.* You will enter the continent of Europe and, in conjunction with the other United Nations, undertake operations aimed at the heart of Germany and the destruction of her armed forces. The date for entering the Continent is the month of May 1944. After adequate Channel ports have been secured, exploitation will be directed towards securing an arena that will facilitate both ground and air operations against the enemy.

3. Notwithstanding the target date above you will be prepared at any time to take immediate advantage of favorable circumstances, such as withdrawal by the enemy on your front, to effect a reentry into the continent with such forces as you have available at the time; a general plan for this operation when approved will be furnished for your assistance.

4. *Command.* You are responsible to the Combined Chiefs of

Staff and will exercise command generally in accordance with the diagram at Appendix. [This is a diagram indicating the chain of command.] Direct communication with the United States and British Chiefs of Staff is authorized in the interest of facilitating your operations and for arranging necessary logistic support.

5. *Logistics.* In the United Kingdom the responsibility for logistics organization, concentration, movement, and supply of forces to meet the requirements of your plan will rest with British service Ministries so far as British Forces are concerned. So far as United States Forces are concerned, this responsibility will rest with the United States War and Navy Departments. You will be responsible for the coordination of logistical arrangements on the continent. You will also be responsible for coordinating the requirements of British and United States forces under your command.

6. *Coordination of operations of other Forces and Agencies.* In preparation for your assault on enemy occupied Europe, Sea and Air Forces, agencies of sabotage, subversion and propaganda, acting under a variety of authorities, are now in action. You may recommend any variation in these activities which may seem to you desirable.

7. *Relationship to United Nations Forces in other Areas.* Responsibility will rest with the Combined Chiefs of Staff for supplying information relating to operations of the Forces of the U.S.S.R. for your guidance in timing your operations. It is understood that the Soviet Forces will launch an offensive at about the same time as OVERLORD with the object of preventing the German forces from transferring from the Eastern to the Western front. The Allied Commander in Chief, Mediterranean Theater, will conduct operations designed to assist your operation including the launching of an attack against the south of France at about the same time as OVERLORD. The scope and timing of his operations will be decided by the Combined Chiefs of Staff. You will establish contact with him

and submit to the Combined Chiefs of Staff your views and recommendations regarding operations from the Mediterranean in support of your attack from the United Kingdom. The Combined Chiefs of Staff will place under your command the forces operating in Southern France as soon as you are in a position to assume such command. You will submit timely recommendations compatible with this regard.

8. *Relationship with Allied Governments—the reestablishment of Civil Governments and Liberated Allied Territories and the administration of enemy territories.* Further instructions will be issued to you on these subjects at a later date.

The wording of this directive fixed on one man the responsibility for its execution. With the assistance of a staff who acted as an extension of his mind, it was General Eisenhower's burden to weigh recommendations and then make his decisions. They were never easy. Ground, air, and naval commanders were all strong men, with strong opinions reinforced by demonstrated professional ability. When I was a young officer, I once heard it said that the loneliest post in the world was that of a commander of a fleet about to go into battle. Yet I have never known a lonelier decision than General Eisenhower was forced to make when he ordered the invasion to proceed. The drama of the unique responsibility which he carried that early morning makes a scene which will never leave my memory. The commanders who surrounded him could only express opinions, yet they were the highest tactical commanders of the forces which would make the assault. Theirs was the responsibility of carrying out the order which he alone could give, and, when his decision was announced, they would have no course but to carry it out with all their heart and skill.

A staff at this high level is also composed of men who have demonstrated outstanding professional ability, and they are entitled, indeed, required, to give their honest estimates of the course which should be followed. Their views may differ from the one which the commander appears to favor. In advance of the final decision, it is the duty of a staff officer to express freely this difference of view. Once the decision is made, he accepts it completely, as though it were his own.

I have recounted one grave expression of such a difference in the first of these narratives. Air Chief Marshal Sir Trafford Leigh-Mallory, General Eisenhower's able air commander, counseled against employing two American airborne divisions behind Utah Beach in the invasion of Normandy. Earlier, Leigh-Mallory had expressed his fear that these divisions would suffer 80 per cent losses in their air drop. A few days before the invasion he repeated his forebodings to General Eisenhower in a letter, forcing the Supreme Commander again to weigh all the factors involved in the face of this expert advice.

The decision was made by General Eisenhower in his advance command post near Portsmouth. He retired alone into his tent to weigh the factors involved. First was his conviction that the assault on Utah Beach could not succeed without the drop of the airborne divisions to secure the exits from the beaches. Second was the belief he had held from his first examination of the invasion plan that without the Utah Beach landing to gain immediately the base of the Cotentin Peninsula the entire operation was too hazardous to attempt. Third, his own judgment denied that the enemy was capable of inflicting the heavy losses his air commander predicted. He confirmed that the drop would take place as planned.

Another incident of this sort comes to mind from the days of the Malta Conference which took place in January, 1945, just in advance of the Yalta meeting of the heads of state. In view of the pressures of the battlefield, General Eisenhower felt he could not attend and sent me to represent him. We were then just regrouping after the German Ardennes counteroffensive and were about to carry through the slashing campaigns west of the Rhine which we believed would destroy a considerable portion of Hitler's remaining effectives before we were ready to storm the river barrier.

In early January General Eisenhower had discussed these campaigns with Field Marshal Sir Alan Brooke, Chief of the British Imperial General Staff. Field Marshal Brooke had presented objections on the ground that the proposed operations would cause a dispersal of our forces and a diversion of necessary divisions from the northern crossing of the Rhine by Field Marshal Montgomery's forces aimed at the Ruhr.

At Malta during a private conversation Sir Alan reiterated these views to me in such positive terms that I informed him I had no choice but to feel he had less confidence in the Supreme Commander than the situation demanded. It would be my duty, I told him, to repeat our conversation and to ask the Conference on the following day to reaffirm its confidence in the Supreme Commander in order that he might be sure of having freedom of action. I am glad to say that the matter was quickly resolved next day. And a few weeks later, when Field Marshal Brooke stood on the banks of the Rhine with General Eisenhower to witness the crossing by troops of the 21st Army Group, he said to General Eisenhower, "You were completely right and I am sorry if my fear of dispersed effort added to your burdens. Thank God you stuck by your guns!"

I cite these two incidents only to show how grave is the responsibility of a supreme commander in the face of differences of opinion by important advisers. At such a time, he can do no more than to retire "into his tent" and assess the bases of decision. He has finished with advice. Now he must make the decision alone, in full realization of the lives that have been entrusted to him and the safety of nations that may hang on his judgment.

It is in this light that the decisions described in the chapters which follow must be considered. At this far distance, with the hindsight of our decisive victory, their importance might seem to fade into the haze of history. But let no one forget the gravity and the urgency of each one when it was made or the colossal strength of the war machine which carried them into effect.

Preparations for the invasion of Normandy were on a scale and of a magnitude far beyond that required by any military expedition that has ever been conceived. The Allied Expeditionary Force was proposing to storm a fortress wall which its German defenders boasted was impregnable. To reach the wall we must transport thousands of men in thousands of ships across the treacherous waters of the English Channel. To the dangers of the assault itself had to be added the hazards of wind and wave. We knew the Channel could be an implacable enemy capable of delivering us as disastrous a blow afloat as we should encounter from the German guns when we rushed the beaches. At headquarters in England, a massive part of the planners' attention had to be directed to the problems of overcoming this preliminary obstacle.

The selection of the Calvados coast of Normandy for the assault had been the recommendation of the planners in Norfolk House. There was no reason to question it. They had been thorough in their consideration. Since the invasion would be mounted from England, they had divided the European coast into six parts and considered each in detail. First, and always most persuasive on the map, was the Pas de Calais area directly across from Dover. This is by far the shortest crossing of the Channel and therefore it is nearest to the airfields in Britain from which our air cover would fly. The German generals expected that we would choose to assault here, and it was in this area that they had concentrated their heaviest defenses.

To the east of this area lay the North Sea coast of Holland and Belgium, still heavily fortified. The planners felt this was too far from British airfields to allow our fighter planes and fighter-bombers an effective scope. In addition, although the beaches here are wide and attractive to the eye, on many the sand is soft. It would present an obstacle to tanks and heavy vehicles carrying supply.

To the west of the Pas de Calais lies the mouth of the Seine, and this was also a possibility. We might land here near Le Havre, with a chance of getting that fine port, but to assault here also meant going ashore on both sides of the Seine's wide mouth. With our initial forces divided by this water obstacle, there was too great a chance that the Germans could concentrate on destroying first one and then the other force, bringing disaster to our entire expedition before we had secured a lodgement area. In addition, the harbor defenses of Le Havre were formidable, and their heavy guns could be brought to bear on our ships and landing craft as they came ashore. Finally, we knew that commanders in all the ports had been ordered to destroy their installations if surrender became inevitable. We should get little immediate assistance from Le Havre in the great build-up of men and supplies which must be accomplished with urgency if our landings were to succeed.

This same consideration caused the planners to discard quickly any thought of assaulting on the coast of the Bay of Biscay. Though this western coast offered excellent ports—Brest, Lorient, St. Nazaire, all the way south to Bordeaux—the Germans would have made sure to destroy them before they fell into our hands. In addition, the beaches there were small and rocky and would have made it difficult to bring ashore an assault

force in the strength we thought necessary to meet the
expected counterattack. Moreover, the air distance from
England was prohibitive.

One by one all of these landing sites were discarded
by the planners in favor of the strip of Calvados coast
running from Caen on the east across the Cotentin Peninsula on the west. This area included the great port of
Cherbourg. Undoubtedly the Germans would render
this unusable until extensive clearing and rebuilding
could be completed, but in the meantime we could provide our own artificial harbors to funnel supply across
the beaches. The beaches themselves on this coast were
wide enough to permit landing the five divisions we intended to use in our initial assault and solid enough to
carry our heavy transport. There were serviceable exits
inland, and while the sea voyage and the air distance
from Britain would be considerably longer than that
across the Strait of Dover to Calais, this was compen-
sated for by certain definite advantages.

Important among these was the fact that this area had
never been so heavily fortified as others along the Channel coast. Confident that we would choose the Pas de
Calais for our assault, the Normandy area was largely
neglected until the early months of 1944. Rommel was
put in command of the Atlantic Wall defenses at this
time and, with his usual energy and skill, he immediately
ordered that the defenses be built up. Because of shortages of steel and concrete, he was hampered in carrying
out his intentions, but it was due to his industry that
new guns began to appear along the heights overlook-

ing the coast, that the beaches were sown with mines, and that obstacles extended right down into the water. Nevertheless, the defenses were never as strong as Rommel intended they should be made.

Another factor, too, gave this area the logic of choice. As the northwest corner of France, it was not only furthest from the enemy's principal supply bases, but because of our superiority in the air we could most effectively isolate the battlefield and make reinforcement difficult. By destroying the bridges over the Seine and Loire just before our attack we could force time-consuming circuitous marches on enemy units which would increase their vulnerability to our rocket-firing fighter-bombers. By this means we intended to wall off our lodgement area from heavy reinforcement by enemy divisions until our strength was adequate for the breakthrough.

For the success of our build-up on the Calvados shore we relied heavily on ingenious installations proposed first, I believe, by Lord Louis Mountbatten to provide artificial harbors on the exposed beaches. These went by the code names of "mulberry" and "gooseberry." The gooseberry was simply a protected anchorage formed by sinking old merchant ships in a line so that an unloading area behind offered relatively calm water. The mulberries were complete harbors in themselves, built in Great Britain, towed by tugs to the Norman coast and sunk in place. Their individual elements were enormous hollow structures of reinforced concrete, which reminded me, when I first saw them, of nothing so much as a six-story building lying on its side. Several such elements constituted a "mulberry." This was an enterprise of formidable size, and some nineteen thousand workmen were engaged on their construction in England. Two "mulberry" harbors were set up, one on the British and the other on the American front. The service they performed was priceless during the early days before we had taken Cherbourg and could begin to repair and use that great port. By D plus 11, we had put ashore 587,653 men and 89,728 vehicles!

The speed and extent of this build-up were far beyond the Germans' calculations of our capabilities, because they did not know about our artificial harbors. Their intelligence had not identified them as they lay in harbor at Selsey Bay before the start of their cross-Channel passage. They were quite unprepared for the power we were able to put into our attacks in Normandy.

To be sure, the Germans were still peering out anxiously from behind their heavy guns in the Pas de Calais, expecting each day to see the ships of our mythical "1st Army Group" looming up out of the Channel mists. Originally, General Bradley had been commander in fact of the 1st Army Group. Later, as part of our plans of deception, his command had been renamed the 12th Army Group, the designation it carried throughout the war. But every effort was made to convince the Germans that the 1st Army Group still existed as a formidable fighting force, and they were allowed to learn that it was commanded by General Patton. A radio network was established for this headquarters, and dummy operational orders flowed over it. Some divisions which we believed the enemy must have identified as being in England were mentioned as part of this group. Others, whose designations were allowed to leak, existed only on paper.

In addition to radio deception, concentrations of shipping and troops were established in the southeastern part of England close to Dover, a fact which we expected the German reconnaissance planes to note in their photographs. Dummy landing craft began to appear in great numbers in the Thames and other waters of this area. Troops, intended for the Normandy operation, were originally quartered here and, when they were moved west for the actual invasion, activity was maintained in the camps, smoke rose from the cooking fires, transport was maintained in the camps' roads, and forces of dummy tanks were clearly visible for the Germans to photograph from high in the air. These devices were largely the result of British ingenuity, and I came to recognize that the British are masters of this sort of deception. All of it played a part in keeping the Germans convinced that another massive attack was coming out from the Dover area to strike at the Pas de Calais.

It seems incredible, considering the hazards, how successful we were in keeping the enemy from learning where we intended to strike. But the special precautions were thorough. In effect, all the exits from England to the outside world were sealed off. Civilian travel between Great Britain and Ireland was halted on February 9. This seemed a necessary measure, since neutral Eire had plenty of Axis agents working quite openly. Beginning on April 1, visitors were excluded from the coastal areas in southern England. A ten-mile strip was placed off-limits to all who had no official business in the area. In the middle of April, the British Government placed restrictions on the activities of diplomatic missions. Diplomats and couriers were forbidden to leave or enter the United Kingdom. And diplomatic mail, ordinarily free from inspection, was censored. Beginning May 25, all mail from American personnel to the United States or elsewhere was subjected to a ten-day delay.

Those last days of May the staff at SHAEF was watching the completion of its five months of ceaseless effort to mount the invasion force. The final great moves were under way. One of the most intricate pieces of planning was now put in execution when the schedules prepared by the combined Army and Navy headquarters began to send troops to the ports in southern England. It was a marvel of inspired timing which brought these thousands of soldiers and their mass of transport to the Channel without attracting undue attention.

Then it was June, and we were with General Eisenhower at the forward command post he had established near Portsmouth. Whatever happened now, we knew that everything was ready. The agonizing threats of shortages in vital landing craft and matériel had been met. For these next few days, our principal enemy was the weather. If General Eisenhower made the decision to go, it would start a mighty offensive that would halt only when Hitler's forces were destroyed and our Allied armies stood victorious in the heart of the Reich.

1. The Invasion Tide

LOOKING back on the war in Europe, six decisions stand out from the tensions of those months as the determining points where the defeat of Hitler was sealed. All were made by the Supreme Allied Commander, General of the Army Dwight D. Eisenhower, on whose shoulders rested the responsibility of every undertaking. The daily routine of our high headquarters was a succession of plan and decision, each vital since it brought us closer to victory. But in these six can be traced the logic of our progress from the ports of England to the final surrender at Reims.

All but the first were based on strictly military considerations, bold decisions which displayed General Eisenhower's unusually keen sense of strategy and timing. The first, on which all others depended, was forced on the Supreme Commander not by the action of the enemy but by the weather.

This was the irrevocable order, issued shortly after 0400 hours on June 5, 1944, to launch the invasion of

Normandy during a twenty-four-hour break in the worst June weather the always uncertain English Channel had churned up in twenty years. We were at Portsmouth, where an advanced command post had been set up overlooking the harbor. Everything the planners could do to insure the success of the gigantic undertaking had been completed. The troops were in the armada's five thousand ships, ready to converge on Normandy from every port in England. Weather could wreck the expedition and already the assault had been postponed a day because of the Channel gale. No commander has ever faced a more formidable decision than General Eisenhower at that dawn meeting of his commanders in chief and meteorologists. With the wind blowing rain against the window, it was one man's responsibility to weigh all the factors and decide—twenty-four hours before H-hour on the beaches—whether he would give the order to go.

When General Eisenhower was appointed Supreme Commander of the Allied Expeditionary Force to cross the Channel and destroy the German armies in western Europe, we were still at our headquarters in North Africa. The appointment was confirmed by President Roosevelt himself on December 7, 1943. I was to continue as his chief of staff. But planning for OVERLORD, code name for the European operation, was already well started under the direction of Lt. Gen. Sir Frederick E. Morgan. At the Casablanca Conference in January, 1943, General Morgan was appointed Chief of Staff to

the Supreme Allied Commander, though it was eleven
months before a supreme commander was selected. The
initials of the new designation spelled out COSSAC, and
COSSAC became the code name of the headquarters in
London which went into business at Norfolk House in
St. James's Square.

In North Africa General Eisenhower had just time
for a brief study of the COSSAC plan before a hurried
trip home to confer with General Marshall and the Combined Chiefs of Staff in Washington. While he approved
the general strategy and the area selected for assault, he
felt the three divisions COSSAC had allotted for the
landings, with two more in the immediate follow-up,
were not enough to storm the beaches against the formidable defenses the Germans had prepared.

"I'd like to assault with twelve divisions if I could,"
he told Field Marshal Montgomery, who was to command all ground forces in the initial phase. He was re-
signed to the fact that the shortage of landing craft,
which had plagued him so gravely during the Salerno
landings, would never permit an assault with twelve
divisions. "But I must have at least five," he insisted.
"Five divisions in the first assault and two to follow up."

He thought, too, that for five divisions the beaches
chosen were too narrow. Since Field Marshal Montgomery and I were to precede him to London, he directed us
to study the OVERLORD plan in detail and do our best to
work out these changes.

I flew to England in early January and went directly
to the headquarters of General Morgan, an old friend

from the planning days of the North African expedition who would remain as Deputy Chief of Staff when I took over for General Eisenhower. He showed me the OVERLORD preparations, and my first reaction was one of absolute astonishment. Not only had great strides been made, but I was amazed at the courage and imagination shown by the War Cabinet and all the planning agencies. Bold and novel measures had been improvised to overcome the obstacles we should encounter in the invasion and build-up of men and supplies in France. On the following morning, Field Marshal Montgomery met the air and naval commanders and the COSSAC staff. Then the general review of plans began.

The exhaustive requirements of staff planning for an operation like OVERLORD are almost unbelievable. It is the job of the staff to keep the commander constantly up-to-date on everything which may conceivably affect his over-all decisions. This includes not only the situation of his own forces but an estimate of the enemy's capabilities and probable intentions as well. The staff develops plans for all operations. In preparing OVERLORD, the staff at Supreme Headquarters issued directives on which detailed plans were submitted by ground, air, and naval commanders to cover their responsibilities in every campaign. These were not only the tactical plans of maneuver but also supply plans listing the weapons, ammunition, and equipment needed and charting their flow to the men at the front. All these plans were assembled, studied, and criticized by the staff at Supreme Headquarters till they were in such shape that the complete master plan could be submitted to General Eisenhower for his decision.

Staff work in war is exacting business. If judgment is faulty in any major particular, the issue on the battlefield is in peril. If the staff overlooks any detail in the enemy's situation or its own armies' needs, a promising victory may be turned into a bitter defeat. A staff lives constantly by Ben Franklin's maxim: "For want of a nail the shoe was lost, for want of a shoe the horse was lost, for want of a horse the rider was lost." For want of good staff work the war could be lost.

During my first days in London, I began to develop the staff at Supreme Headquarters along the lines General Eisenhower wanted. It was to be a fully integrated Allied staff like the one which had planned and directed our operations in the Mediterranean. Nationality was completely disregarded. Already, under General Morgan, the staff was about evenly divided between American and British officers, but the uniform a man wore had been no consideration in his selection. I proposed to keep it that way. As time went on, a few officers were relieved—not many—and replaced by others who seemed more imaginative or better suited to produce under pressure the results we must have. In deference to the nationality of the Supreme Commander, we substituted American for British staff methods. This caused minor confusion at first, but our British officers soon became accustomed to American procedure and liked it.

Our earliest concern was to find a practical solution of General Eisenhower's desire to increase the assault force and widen the invasion beaches. Careful re-examination of the data assembled by the COSSAC planners confirmed their opinion that the area selected was the one where, from all points of view, we were likely to get ashore with minimum losses. The Normandy beaches had just enough capacity to allow an increase in the assaulting force to five divisions, provided we were prepared to accept some added difficulties. Utah Beach, the area added to the American sector on the shoulder of the Cotentin Peninsula, would be separated from Omaha Beach to the east by the Carentan Estuary, so that the forces could not be mutually supporting till a link-up was made further inland. Worse still, a large flooded area behind this beach constituted a formidable obstacle to overcome.

General Eisenhower reviewed the proposed changes when he returned to England on January 15 and expressed himself as satisfied. He was anxious to spend as much time as possible familiarizing himself with the detailed COSSAC plan and then to call a meeting of his deputies and commanders in chief where the whole operation of the assault could be discussed. He wanted to be sure of wholehearted support of his proposed revisions, and we set up a conference for January 21 at Norfolk House.

The meeting was something of an historic occasion. It brought together for the first time in their new assignments the men who would direct the over-all strategy and tactics responsible for Germany's defeat in the West. It secured agreement on the only major revisions which were to be made in plans for the cross-Channel assault. As an added bit of interest, these British and American allies were meeting in an atmosphere of the utmost cordiality on the site of the birthplace of George III.

There was little need for introductions when General Eisenhower entered. Almost every man present was an old friend, tried and tested in previous Allied undertakings. Air Chief Marshal Sir Arthur W. Tedder had been Air Commander in Chief in the Mediterranean and would be Deputy Supreme Commander for the new operation. Admiral Sir Bertram H. Ramsay, Commander in Chief of the Allied Naval Expeditionary Force, directed much of the naval planning for the landings in North Africa. Air Chief Marshal Sir Trafford Leigh-Mallory, Commander in Chief of the Allied Air Expeditionary Force, was new to most of us but well known by reputation. It is sad to recall that both these fine officers who played so outstanding a part in our victory lost their lives before the war ended.

Field Marshal Sir Bernard L. Montgomery, as Commander of the 21st Army Group, would direct all ground forces during the initial phase of the landings and build-up of the Continent. Lt. Gen. Omar N. Bradley commanded the American First Army, now a part of 21st Army Group. Later, as our forces increased, he would have command of an independent American army group in France.

General Eisenhower's decisions for increasing the strength and power of the assault were accepted enthusiastically. On only one point was a question voiced.

General Eisenhower intended to use two American airborne divisions to secure our landings at Utah Beach on the Cotentin Peninsula. His reasons were compelling. Behind the landing area stretched the low ground the Germans had flooded. A few roads crossed the marshy, mile-wide strip, but unless airborne troops were put down on the firm ground behind to seize the roadheads and engage the defenders, the narrow causeways across the marshes could be raked by enemy fire. Our troops would take heavy casualties forcing their way inland from the beaches.

Because of strong antiaircraft defenses in the area, Air Chief Marshal Leigh-Mallory was dubious about the success of such an undertaking. He was also doubtful that suitable drop zones could be found in the relatively small area in which the airborne divisions must be placed. The airborne commanders and their staffs were much more confident after a thorough study, but Leigh-Mallory remained unconvinced. In the end, General Eisenhower was forced to confirm the operation over the still strongly opposed view of his air commander in chief.

A few days before the invasion itself, Leigh-Mallory reiterated his honest conviction of heavy losses. He felt they might run as high as 75 per cent or even higher. In the opinion of General Eisenhower and his principal ground commanders, the airborne landing was so vital to the outcome of our assault that to cancel it would endanger the whole success of our offensive. Neither he nor the staff shared the gloomy view of the air commander in chief. It is a matter of record that losses to the airborne elements in the first drop were less than 2 per cent. Total losses for the entire operation were less than 10 per cent.

One other important matter was agreed on at this meeting—postponement of the target date of the invasion by a month. Originally it had been ordered by the Combined Chiefs of Staff for May 1, but another month was essential to round up the large number of additional landing craft, and naval supporting and convoy vessels required, as well as to complete the administrative planning necessary to load, land, and supply the increased force. Five initial infantry divisions and two in the follow-up meant that a total of seven divisions must be loaded in assault boats on D-Day. A threatening shortage of landing craft and supporting warships continued to hang over the operation till late in March, when we were finally assured of the full number we should need.

With a soldier's impatience of cities when operations are to be planned, one of General Eisenhower's first orders was to move the staff out of London. General Spaatz made room for us at his headquarters, Bushy Park, near Kingston-on-Thames, and we completed the move in early March. Not entirely in secrecy as it developed. The late Lord Haw-Haw wished us well in our new surroundings a few days after we were installed.

Shuttling between Bushy Park and conferences in London, the advancing spring required a never-ending series of decisions by the Supreme Commander, some minor but others reached only after the most grave deliberation. Often one or both of us attended sessions of the War Cabinet at 10 Downing Street, presided over by the Prime Minister with his customary vigor. These meetings usually began at ten in the evening and continued till two or three in the morning. It was there that we discussed, not once but many times, the decision General Eisenhower had reached to bomb French rail centers to isolate the battle area in Normandy and hinder the enemy's efforts to bring up men and supplies.

The military necessity of attacking these targets was apparent from the war map. In January the German divisions strung along the Channel coast from Holland to Brittany numbered fifty. Our Intelligence constantly tracked additional divisions from positions further south to the critical area. In the first days ashore we should have lean resources compared to the Germans. We must seize every means to reduce the enemy's power to build up a counterattack.

Set against this was the certainty that to bomb French rail centers would cause the death of many French civilians. It might even alienate the people of France. With these troubling possibilities in mind, the War Cabinet urged General Eisenhower to reconsider. General Koenig, who commanded from England the French Forces of the Interior, added a protest. The decision was not easily adhered to in the face of these earnest pleas, but the stern logic of General Eisenhower's conviction finally prevailed.

I shall not soon forget the expression on the face of General Koenig when I talked with him about these bombings. As a Frenchman, he was torn by the additional suffering they would cause his people. But as a soldier, he recognized the vital military part they would play in the liberation of France. I doubt if the expression "C'est la guerre" was ever used with deeper feeling. The bombings began two months before the invasion, and by leaflets and other warnings we managed to get French civilians away from the targets. Casualties were far lower than had been feared. Of the confusion the shattered rail lines caused the Germans, we had eloquent evidence on the battlefield. Units straggled into the combat area without their heavy equipment and after circuitous night marches. Allied planes made the roads sudden death by day.

Other strategic bombing decisions were taken. As invasion preparations were stepped up, aircraft and oil became the all-important targets. In January the air campaign began which whittled the German air force to a shaky ghost of its former power. Three weeks before D-Day, we began a systematic bombing of all airfields within 130 miles of the battle area to keep fighter opposition to a minimum during the assault.

In spite of these intensive attacks, we expected the Luftwaffe to appear for a noisy Götterdämmerung. We knew the Germans had reserves hidden away out of reach of our own bombers. Knowing also their boast that we would never gain a foothold on shore, we were quite prepared to have them bring out every weapon in their arsenal to smash our assault.

Goering explained, when he fell into our hands at the end of the war, why his fighters and bombers were not ordered to their immolation over the invasion armada. Under our destructive pounding, the Luftwaffe had declined to a sad state by D-Day, he told us. The fact was, he said, to send his bombers to battle with the enormously superior Allied air force would have been frank suicide, and he chose to nurse them cautiously for night mine-laying operations off the beaches which might hamper our build-up. To explode his remaining reserves of fighters into the midst of our squadrons would quite clearly mean their destruction, too. At the very outset of the Battle of France, Germany would have been left without a fighter force in the Luftwaffe.

That winter and spring there was a new primary target—the strange installations clustered in the Pas de Calais which were to be the launching sites for V weapons. We watched their construction anxiously and bombed them from their first appearance. The Air Ministry was certain they were closely connected with the secret weapons of which Hitler continually boasted. But the missiles were so long in coming that some of our officers—highly placed, too—advanced the theory that the platforms were a gigantic hoax, constructed by the Nazis with great cunning to divert our bombers from vital targets.

The storm of buzz bombs did not break till a week after the invasion was launched. Then London felt the dread of sudden disaster. We were hit several times at Bushy Park, and a direct hit in London wiped out at one stroke the greater part of one of our Air Intelligence sections. Our greatest fear was that the flying bombs would be directed toward the ports of southern England, where our flotillas were loading men and supplies for the build-up in Normandy. We have only Hitler's unreasoning hatred to thank that the great majority were sited on London.

No one who lived through that time of tension could fail to have deep admiration for the fortitude of the Londoners or sympathy for their suffering under this weapon of destruction. One Sunday afternoon shortly after the invasion the Prime Minister paid a special visit all alone to our headquarters to ask General Eisenhower, wistfully, how soon he expected Allied ground troops would overrun the launching sites. There was little the Supreme Commander could give him in the way of immediate comfort. Mr. Churchill knew the military plan. Our strategy did not lead at once to the area where the sites were located.

He nodded as General Eisenhower reminded him. London could take it, he asserted stoutly, adding with his usual bulldog courage that nothing must jeopardize the success of our offensive. Only, he said, as soon as the critical launching area could reasonably come into the sphere of military operations, would Ike make personally certain there was no delay in stopping this hideous destruction? To that the Commander could heartily pledge his word.

By April, most of the great decisions concerning OVERLORD had been taken—except the final climactic one of the exact day when the invasion would be launched. Now, with most of the planning behind, General Eisenhower was restless for an advanced command post on the channel where he could get the feel of this vast power he directed. We found a good site in the patches of wood which crowned the bluff overlooking Portsmouth Harbor, not far from Southwick House where Admiral Ramsay had his headquarters. Here we set up tents and trailers and went into bivouac with the advance echelon of the staff which would move to France as soon as we had elbow room. Main headquarters remained at Bushy Park, but more and more, as the invasion date approached, General Eisenhower was at Portsmouth.

During April, the first of the meetings was set up to drill the Supreme Commander in the weather factors that would govern his invasion decision. These "dry runs" were held weekly at first, then semiweekly and finally, after the first of June, there were three meetings each day. From the beginning it had been clear that the choice of D-Day depended on the weather. We proposed to cross the treacherous waters of the English Channel with more than five thousand ships and hundreds of smaller ship-to-shore craft to assault a coast bristling with determined troops and all manner of fixed defenses. The hazardous expedition would hang on four factors of weather.

First, we wanted low tide so that the underwater and half-hidden beach obstacles could be seen and destroyed by our demolition crews. The low tide must be late enough in the morning for an hour's good daylight to permit the saturation bombing of defenses which would precede the landings themselves. But it must come early enough in the morning so that a second low tide would occur before darkness set in. Without the second low tide we could not land the follow-up divisions.

For the airborne landings behind Utah Beach and at road centers around Caen, timed for 0200 hours on D-Day, we needed a late-rising full moon so the pilots could approach their objectives in darkness but have moonlight to pick out the drop zones. For the naval craft and transports, we must have a reasonable sea and good visibility to reduce the perils of navigation in crowded waters and to keep troops from arriving at the point of assault so seasick they could not leave their ships. Finally, we hoped for a fair wind blowing inshore to drive the smoke and dust of battle toward the enemy.

Two of these requirements were within the ready prediction of the meteorologists. They could tell us when we should have the low tide and the full moon. During four days in early June, they said, the exact conditions—barring storms—would be forthcoming: on the fourth, fifth, sixth, and seventh. The ideal day was June 5. But of the other critical factors—wind, sea, and storm—the experts could give no certain prediction. Those were in the hands of fate.

It was foolhardy to imagine that all the conditions would be perfect. The dry runs were to accustom the Supreme Commander to estimating the minimum he could accept. The meetings were held first at Bushy Park and later in Southwick House at Portsmouth, attended by the three commanders in chief—Admiral

Ramsay, Field Marshal Montgomery, and Air Chief Marshal Leigh-Mallory, with their chiefs of staff. The meteorologists were two American and two British officers headed by Group Captain J. M. Stagg, a tall, quiet, blue-eyed Scotsman who was their chief.

The weather men produced their calculations for the period twenty-four hours away, since General Eisenhower would have to make his final decision at least that far in advance. They predicted the ceiling and the amount of cloud, the direction and velocity of the wind, and the nature of the sea. Then General Eisenhower and each of his commanders asked questions. When everything was complete in his mind, the Supreme Commander weighed the weather factors one against the other and made his practice decision—to launch the invasion next day or to postpone it.

The time was fast approaching when the decision would be taken in all seriousness. On May 17, General Eisenhower tentatively set D-Day for June 5.

By April the invasion fleet began to assemble. Portsmouth filled with vessels of every description—battleships, destroyers, minesweepers, transports, and hundreds of landing craft. Nosed rail to rail, they opened their jaws to receive cargoes of men and vehicles and guns. Then the khaki flood began. Troops streamed off the roads and fanned out along the macadamed hards which stretched down to the water as far as the eye could reach. Gradually, bits and pieces of the gigantic assault mechanism slipped into place.

Furtive German reconnaissance planes flew over

Portsmouth and the other loading ports. We knew the photographs they made would be eagerly scanned across the Channel for clues to our intentions. We could not conceal these preparations. We could only hope the enemy did not learn—or guess—the exact place and time.

The curious thing is that Hitler did guess the approximate place, so we were told later by General Walther Warlimont, Deputy Chief of the German Armed Forces Staff, rated as one of the best of the enemy planners. In May we noticed that Normandy was being reinforced around the base of the Cotentin Peninsula. According to Warlimont, it was May 2 when Hitler's busy intuition spurred him to order that antiaircraft and antitank weapons be increased all through Normandy and Brittany. He was sure we would attack in Normandy, basing his guess both on the British areas where our troops were concentrated and a sudden conviction that our strategy would be to land near Cherbourg. The German High Command was unanimous in believing that we would try to seize a port quickly to speed our build-up. On May 4, Hitler ordered a parachute division transferred from the Eastern front to Normandy and moved up one of the last of his reserve divisions from Germany. Rommel's panzer divisions were also deployed in May so they could mass on Normandy.

"Up to May, 1944, when Hitler first spoke of Normandy," Warlimont said, "the staff was all prepared for a landing in the Channel zone between the Seine and the

Somme, by Abbeville and Le Havre. Therefore, throughout 1942 and 1943 the coastal defenses were mainly built up in that area. We were not quite convinced that Hitler was right in expecting the attack in Normandy, but he kept harping on it and demanded more and more reinforcements for that sector."

The German generals believed the attack would come east of the Seine because it offered the shortest route across the Channel and the shortest way to Germany and the Ruhr. They also felt we would want to attack in that region because our air force could give better support close to its British bases. But Hitler held to his belief that Normandy was the place. "We generals figured along the lines of our regular military education," Warlimont observed, "but Hitler figured, as he always did, out of intuition." Strangely enough, except for the reinforcements of troops and weapons no special alert was given to the forces in Normandy, so Warlimont said. The High Command was quite confident that our assault could be thrown back, wherever it came.

The key to the German strategy for defending Fortress Europa lay in the formidable defenses of the Atlantic Wall and the lack of any prepared line of fortifications behind it. In our reconnaissance photographs, visualized on immense relief maps showing every contour and every gun on the Norman coast, the German plan was revealed.

Their Atlantic Wall was to be treated as a fortress, which no invader must be permitted to breach. Heavy guns were emplaced in massive concrete casemates to bear on the invasion fleet at sea. Supporting these were strongpoints with machine guns sited to pour cross fire on the beaches as the landing craft came in.

Field Marshal Erwin Rommel had been assigned by Hitler to the job of putting the final touches to the defenses about the same time General Eisenhower was named Supreme Commander. Very soon we saw the results of Rommel's driving energy. In February, new beach obstacles began appearing, strung down into the water itself. These consisted of wood and steel stakes driven into the bottom of "hedgehogs," twisted formations of heavy steel bars, and of "Element C," an obstacle which resembled a huge steel gate. Many of the obstacles were mined. The beaches were strung with barbed wire and mined, although not so thickly as Rommel had ordered, so prisoners of war told us later. German naval authorities assured the High Command, we also learned, that no craft could come ashore through this formidable field.

Except for the single worry of the weather, we were never concerned about our ability to penetrate the Atlantic Wall. Measures had been designed to overcome every hazard we could foresee. Studying the German strategy, we estimated that it would make our landings difficult but give us fairly easy going for a time, once the wall was breached. Landing parties, sent over almost nightly to some section of the Channel coast, brought back intelligence on the gun positions. Exact targets were assigned in advance, not only to the strategic and tactical bombers but to naval guns of the fleet. Because we had measured the thickness of the concrete casemates, we knew there were some guns which could not be silenced from sea or air. Special units of rangers and commandos were detailed to destroy these by direct assault.

Our principal anxiety in the landings was not the Atlantic Wall but what we believed the Germans would do, once we had demonstrated the vulnerability of their coastal defenses. There is an old military maxim: "When you do not know the intentions of the enemy, assume he will act with good judgment." Good judgment in this case would be to concentrate infantry and panzer divisions for a strong counterattack at the earliest moment. Since the entire German Seventh Army was deployed in the general area of our assault, we knew there was plenty of strength available. Our planners exerted their greatest efforts on two objectives: To speed our own build-up in Normandy, and to keep the Germans from concentrating their forces for a counterattack before we were ready.

The air offensive to cut down the Luftwaffe was part of this campaign. Attacks on rail centers destroyed the principal means of quick reinforcement of the battle area. As a further obstacle, beginning a month and a half before D-Day we concentrated on the bridges over the Seine and the Loire. By June 6, all but two of the Seine bridges below Paris were out, and the remaining ones were destroyed soon after. Most of the bridges over the Loire below Orléans had also been knocked out by our bombing attacks.

In addition to these direct methods, we hoped the

Germans would hesitate to rush reinforcements to Normandy in fear that the assault there was only part of our invasion with other attacks to be expected elsewhere. In this we were successful beyond our most optimistic dreams and, I might add, beyond good military judgment on the part of the German High Command. The Germans acted on the assumption that we would make at least two landings. They thought the invasion fleet off Normandy must represent only half or less of our total offensive force. For six weeks after we were ashore, nineteen badly needed infantry divisions of the Fifteenth German Army were held idle in the Pas de Calais area, where the enemy continued to believe General Patton would land with a second major assault.

We did nothing to disabuse our enemy of this delusion and much to foster it. Dummy landing ships appeared in the Thames and also on the Dover coast, and there were camps in East Anglia which might have bivouacked thousands of troops. Actually they were deserted tent cities, given semblance of life by enough men to keep the fires burning for German reconnaissance pilots to photograph.

There was was one assumption of the German High Command with which I am in thorough agreement: They thought our invasion could not succeed unless we had a port. What the High Command did not know was that we were bringing our port with us. Their Intelligence completely missed what was undoubtedly the most ingenious and fantastic plan ever conceived to overcome lack of port facilities on a hostile shore. This was the string of sheltered anchorages, including two actual harbors each the size of Dover, which we ferried across the Channel piecemeal and assembled opposite the invasion beaches.

The Germans never realized the vital importance of these strange contraptions in the Thames which looked something like six-story office buildings lying on their sides. Laborers who had worked on grain elevators in the north of England hazarded the guess that they were floating grain elevators which we proposed to tow across the Channel to feed the civilian population of Europe. We did not contradict the story. Col. Gen. Alfred Jodl, Chief of the Armed Forces Staff, thought that they were piers designed to replace those we should find demolished if we were lucky enough to get a port. These harbors were the ultimate invention of the Engineers of the War Office, and upon them we pinned our hope of accomplishing the build-up we should need in Normandy to throw back the German counterattack.

Undoubtedly lack of knowledge of these emergency measures contributed to the overconfidence with which the Germans' viewed their ability to throw our landings back into the sea. The High Command badly underestimated our speed in putting troops and supplies ashore. "Not knowing about the artificial ports," General Warlimont told us, "we could not estimate your rate of supply. We were able later to gauge the rate at which you were landing troops but confined ourselves to strength figures, number of divisions, as our reconnaissance did not give us much information on your troops, and still less on your supply circumstances. If you ask why the German Air Force did not bomb the places where you landed more effectively," he added ruefully, "the answer is that our air force was unable to break through your defenses in order to find and hit the targets at all!"

The tension of the last few weeks before the invasion was tightened by shortages which kept threatening in various critical items, requiring urgent cables to Washington. Once it was mortar shells. At another time it was 105 mm ammunition. But all our minimum requirements were filled at last. When the troops were loaded into the invasion fleet, we could congratulate ourselves that they lacked nothing an army could give them to insure the success of their tremendous undertaking.

Mr. Churchill once spoke in a War Cabinet meeting of "the countless hours of work, the enormous amount of time and effort that must be expended by thousands of people, in order that a few brave men can rush on to the beaches of France and plunge their bayonets into the bowels of the enemy." I think that no one who has not been intimately engaged in such a planning task can have any idea of its magnitude. Now it was complete.

The Supreme Commander made the rounds of assaulting divisions and noted with satisfaction that the troops seemed hard and eager. The soft English spring moved toward June in a succession of beautiful days and long twilights which deepened into perfect nights. If the weather held, the Supreme Commander's decision would be a routine confirmation of June 5 as D-Day. It was comforting to remember that General Eisenhower was not only a great commander but a lucky one. Everyone had said so since North Africa, when the calmest seas in the oldest inhabitant's memory bore our first invasion shoreward. His reputation had been confirmed off Sicily when a sudden storm lashed the invasion fleet on its perilous crossing and then miraculously died in time for H-hour on the beaches.

But as May wore out, June dawned dark and stormy with a gale over the Channel. Up at SHIPMATE—code name of the Advanced Command Post on the bluff—we shivered in our tents and trailers. The meteorologists in their Nissen huts near Admiral Ramsay's headquarters worked desperately, searching the fronts for clearer skies. They were not only trying to predict the weather, they were trying to make it. Commanders' meetings at Southwick House were charged with worry. The sober fact was that the worst June storm in twenty years was whipping the Channel.

By 1000 hours on June 3, it was evident that the weather was worsening, not improving. The meteorologists confirmed it. Periodically that day we listened to their forecasts, but they could promise no immediate change. There could be no invasion on June 5—the ideal day. At a special commanders' meeting at 0200 on June 4, General Eisenhower accepted the certainty of delay. After discussing the matter gravely with his commanders, he issued orders to postpone the operation for at least twenty-four hours.

The timetable required slower elements of the fleet to

be in motion well before the major force was launched. Some were already under way. Because radio silence was imperative for the security of our plans, destroyers were dispatched to round them up. That afternoon, the Supreme Commander sent me down to the hards to see the men who came back to Portsmouth. It was heartbreaking to watch their faces. The eagerness had gone out of them, now that the edge of their expectation was dulled. I have never seen more unhappy soldiers.

There was no promise of a break in the weather that evening. With all their alchemy, the weather wizards could not lift the blanket of cloud which hung over our heads and our spirits. We drove back through the blackout after the ten o'clock meeting on June 4 with the dull realization that if we could not go on June 6, we should almost certainly have to postpone our assault for another two weeks, the earliest date when the tide would again be right. Although June 7 would still have met our conditions if the weather had cleared, some of the ships which had come down from northern ports would have insufficient fuel to carry through the assault phase if it were postponed till June 7.

It was still drizzling outside the trailer when I got up to attend the meeting set for 0400 on the morning of June 5. A chill wind blew through the bivouac area, accompanied by little gusts of rain, and I pulled on a sheepskin jacket to keep out the cold. My jeep clattered over the steel matting which kept a bottom in the roads through camp, and I turned into the high road along the bluff which skirts the harbor. The wind was driving clouds across a steely sky, pushing at the barrage balloons which swayed above the ships. I tried to keep thoughts from my mind because there was nothing now that thinking could accomplish. Now it was time for action.

A Royal Marine sentry passed me through the gate at Southwick House. I turned my jeep into the long road which winds between great trees and found the car park in the darkness. The handsome interior of the old manor had been stripped to make way for the tables, desks, and communications equipment which were part of Admiral Ramsay's headquarters. But the library had been left a comfortable room for conferences. It was a little before four when I went in.

There was coffee ready. I took a cup from a young flag lieutenant and moved toward the pleasant fire. All the commanders were there when General Eisenhower arrived, trim in his tailored battle jacket, his face tense with the gravity of the decision which lay before him. Field Marshal Montgomery wore his inevitable baggy corduroy trousers and sweat shirt. Admiral Ramsay and his chief of staff were immaculate in Navy blue and gold.

The meteorologists were brought in at once. There was the ghost of a smile on the tired face of Group Captain Stagg, the tall Scot. "I think we have found a gleam of hope for you, sir," he said to General Eisenhower, and we all listened expectantly. "The mass of weather fronts coming in from the Atlantic is moving faster than we anticipated," the chief meteorologist continued. "We predict there will be rather fair conditions beginning late on June 5 and lasting until the next morning, June 6, with a drop in wind velocity and some break in the clouds. Ceiling—about 3,000."

But toward the evening of June 6, his charts showed, there would be a recurrence of bad weather with high winds and rough seas. It was impossible for the experts to predict how much longer the bad weather would last. They were giving us about twenty-four hours of reasonable weather. That was all.

Rapid questions were asked by all the commanders. Leigh-Mallory wanted to know just how much cloud could be expected for his bombers—ten-ten, eight-ten, six-ten. The forecasters satisfied him. Admiral Ramsay asked about the seas, the strength and velocity of the wind. General Eisenhower inquired how many hours he could count on for the attack and just when bad weather would resume. "The morning will be fair," the Scot said. "Good weather may last through the afternoon."

All the questions had been asked, and then there was silence. No one broke it, and I suppose all the men were thinking, as I was, that postponement now meant two weeks' delay. It meant an almost insoluble problem of what to do with the thousands of troops in the ships. I remembered their dejected faces. It was impossible to keep them closed in for two weeks, yet to let them out of the beach areas would almost certainly convey information to the Germans about our attack. There was the problem of the press correspondents, too—almost a hundred scattered through the invasion force. The very fact that they filed no dispatches for two weeks would arouse suspicion. Finally, there would be the reaction of our Russian ally, whose great Eastern offensive was to be coordinated with our assault on Europe.

The silence lasted for five full minutes while General Eisenhower sat on a sofa before the bookcase which filled the end of the room. I never realized before the loneliness and isolation of a commander at a time when such a momentous decision has to be taken, with full knowledge that failure or success rests on his judgment alone. He sat there quietly, not getting up to pace with quick strides as he often does. He was tense, weighing every consideration of weather as he had been briefed to do during the dry runs since April, and weighing with them those other imponderables.

Finally he looked up, and the tension was gone from his face.

He said briskly, "Well, we'll go!"

SITUATION REPORT

* * * * *

THAT NIGHT of June 5, eve of D-Day, the gliders
and the troop carriers moved out, carrying the airborne troops who would be the first to meet the enemy
on the Far Shore. The British flew east of the Cotentin
Peninsula, then drove directly for their drop zone near
Caen. The American gliders flew that way, too, turning southwest to land beyond the flooded area behind
Utah Beach. The American troop carriers took a course
to the west of the Cotentin, then turned southeast and
the paratroopers dropped on France. The armada carrying troops and their supply plowed through the rough
Channel seas, Engineers attacked the underwater obstacles, and the troops unloaded through heavy surf on
the beaches. On Admiral Kirk's flagship, General Bradley anxiously watched the shore, which was only dimly
visible. At 0550 the *Augusta*'s guns opened fire on the
coastal forts, beginning the general bombardment, and at
0615 the heavy bombers of the Eighth Air Force in
wave after wave dropped their bombs on the defenses.

Rangers and commandos were clambering up the heights to attack the shore batteries of heavily emplaced guns that could not be silenced from the sea. H-Hour came at 0700, and on the beaches the great invasion had begun.

The Supreme Commander was over next day on a fast mine layer to confer aboard ship with his commanders. In the ensuing days he made many trips by sea, and by air as soon as landing strips were in. In early August, General Eisenhower set up his own headquarters in France (code-named SHELLBURST) in an apple orchard near Tournières and Maisons.

In England the flying bombs increased their devastation. SHAEF was concerned that they might disrupt the loading of reinforcements and supply by being directed toward the ports. Hitler preferred to express his hatred of Britain by directing most of them toward London. The artificial harbors went in to speed supply across the Normandy beaches, and there was feverish work in Cherbourg after its capture to repair the extensive demolitions the Germans had carried out. Supply was the key to the advance. The Supreme Commander was up and down the front, constantly urging action to prevent the Germans from digging in and creating a static front.

In mid-August the invasion of southern France came in and began the northward offensive that, by joining up with Third Army on September 21, created a solid Allied front the entire length of France. Marseilles helped to give us desperately needed port facilities. On the evening of August 24, the liberation of Paris began when the French 2nd Armored Division, designated by

General Bradley for this honor, entered the city and accepted the surrender of the German garrison commander. SHAEF Forward was at Granville in Normandy now. On August 1, General Patton had officially taken command of Third Army in Normandy, and his spearheads began darting into Brittany and striking southeastward below Paris. This same day, General Bradley assumed command of the 12th Army Group and turned over his First Army command to General Hodges. The tempo of battle was increasing now, with British and American forces shaken free of their beachhead and out into the open for the war of maneuver they had waited for during the cramped days in the lodgement area. On September 1, General Eisenhower took over tactical command of all ground forces from Field Marshal Montgomery, and on September 15 he also took tactical command of the forces of General Devers, 6th Army Group commander of the troops who had invaded southern France. On September 18, SHAEF Main moved its headquarters from Bushy Park to Versailles and established itself in the building which the Nazi headquarters had evacuated. Now the whole enterprise was on the Far Shore, its advance slowing until supply could catch up, but planning for the campaigns which would bring victory the following May.

2. Normandy Turning Point

USUALLY a high commander's decisions are reached in a headquarters far away from the battlefield. Most of them, in fact, are settled months before the battle itself takes place. But the decision that sealed the final destruction of German forces in northwest France was made by General Eisenhower at the forward headquarters of Lt. Gen. Omar N. Bradley, who had just been elevated to command of the new American 12th Army Group. Out of the pattern of battle had emerged an opportunity for victory in Normandy so decisive that the liberation of all France must follow. It was the result of Hitler's insistence on an old Prussian principle that there is only one line in battle and the line must hold.

Coming two months after the order to launch the invasion of Normandy through a twenty-four-hour break in the worst weather the English Channel had seen in twenty years, it was the second of six great decisions made by the Supreme Commander which assured the annihilation of Germany's military power in the West.

59

This one, in the actual making, comprised little more than a nod of the head, a go-ahead sign to his brilliant lieutenant, Bradley, who had already sketched out in his own mind a plan to take advantage of the glowing opportunity then opening before us. But that nod of the head was the personal assumption of a responsibility that could be assumed by no other. It defied obviously grave risks to secure decisive victory.

Before the invasion, Field Marshal Sir Bernard L. Montgomery, who directed land operations for securing our lodgement area on the Continent, had developed the original scheme of maneuver to bring us fighting out of our Norman corner for the decisive Battle of France. Although tactics always depend to some extent on the strategy of the enemy, his plan, as approved by General Eisenhower, was this: The weight of our attack would first be put at Caen behind the British and Canadian troops who held the eastern flank of the line. Below Caen there were good sites for airfields and favorable ground for the war of maneuver we intended to force on the enemy at the earliest opportunity to exploit our superiority in armor. Meanwhile, the Americans further west would take Cherbourg, secure the port, and then drive down the Cotentin Peninsula. When this maneuver was accomplished, General Bradley's forces would be in position to break through to the south and overrun Brittany. General Patton's Third Army was designed for just this purpose.

Brittany continued to be a major objective throughout most of the campaign until later events canceled its importance to us. We originally intended to use its fine harbors to funnel troops and supplies to the front directly from the United States, as we had in the First World War. Assuming that the Germans would be discouragingly thorough in their demolitions at the principal ports, we planned to develop a great harbor at Quiberon Bay. When Patton could be shaken loose, he was to drive south across the neck of the Brittany peninsula to seize this area about midway up the southern coast.

These plans were based, of course, on our estimate of the defensive strategy we believed the Germans were most likely to adopt. Once the possibility of holding us in Normandy had vanished, we judged that sound military doctrine would impel them to withdraw to prepared positions along the Seine. When Allied pressure squeezed them there, we expected they would fall back in reasonably good order first to the Somme and then to the Siegfried Line. In Africa, Field Marshal Erwin Rommel had proved himself master of the skillful withdrawal maneuver, and Rommel had the field command in Normandy. There was always the possibility that the "conqueror complex," which resists giving up a foot of vassal territory, would intervene and develop a stubbornness that we could exploit. But unless the German High Command made serious blunders, there was little we could do in the planning stage to counter such withdrawals. By D plus 90 in early September, we expected to be out of Normandy and facing the enemy for a bitter battle along the Seine.

General Eisenhower talked earnestly with General Bradley as they studied the map under the apple trees of the Norman orchard. Instead of slow progress across France to the Siegfried Line, Hitler's blind insistence on fighting to the end in Normandy had now opened a new and stimulating prospect of victory. The day was August 10, 1944. The whole front was in a state of upheaval. On the map, the blue designations of the American forces extended solidly down from Cherbourg and around the base of the Peninsula where they met the red lines of the British and Canadians. Along the western coast, the blue sliced through the black lines of the enemy in the narrow corridor between Avranches and the sea —the break-through. Below this embattled town, long, curving lines had begun to trace the rampaging spear-heads of General Patton's tanks.

To the east around Caen, there was a solid base of red symbols which marked the British and Canadian strength of the 21st Army Group. Deep salients punched into the German lines. On this point, since the very first day of our assault, the enemy had massed his strongest forces to prevent a break-through. But this front, too, was now in motion. The Germans, fighting stubbornly, were being pushed southward toward Falaise. Hitler's entire Seventh Army was in peril.

Except for our corridor along the sea, the German line still held, and east of Avranches the map showed a strong movement of German armor around Mortain. Here, for three days, General von Kluge, who now commanded enemy forces in northwest France, had been vainly attacking to cut our slender line of communications and drive a wedge to the sea.

That was the situation which the Supreme Commander had come to discuss. If General Bradley could spare major forces in the face of von Kluge's threat, then the Allied tactical plan would immediately be changed to take advantage of the new opportunity. General Patton's spearhead reaching through Le Mans would be cocked at Argentan, far to the north. Within this outer encirclement, the American First Army could be turned eastward in a swift movement toward the same town, meeting the British forces descending on Falaise and closing giant pincers around the whole of the German Seventh Army. The American commanders found they had both been considering this glittering and quite unexpected goal.

The scale of the opportunity presented to the Supreme Commander at this point justified the boldest risk. To a staff officer, seeing it all in the red, blue, and black symbols on the map, it was almost unbelievable that the German High Command could have let the bulk of its forces in France be maneuvered into such a desperate position. Our Third Army spearheads were swung on the wide encirclement. Once it was completed, the Germans could not extricate themselves. They still had a brief time when the way to the Seine was open behind them. But the incredible fact remained that they had made no preparations to form a strong secondary defense line anywhere in France. Our air intelligence, sweeping as far as the Westwall, confirmed it. There were no well-prepared positions on the Seine. There were none further east along the Somme. With disaster impending, the German Seventh Army seemed deliberately to invite its own destruction.

We thought then that their lack of air reconnaissance over our lines might have kept full knowledge of their perilous situation from them. In all truth, they were fighting blind. But that seemed an insufficient explanation for what was about to happen, while the enemy counterattacked west instead of withdrawing east. General Bradley was not disturbed about his local situation, particularly in view of the high promise of the new offensive. If the Germans succeeded in cutting through temporarily, the Supreme Commander pointed out that our armor below the break could be supplied with two thousand tons a day by air.

With that much settled, General Bradley communicated with Field Marshal Montgomery, who was still responsible for direction of operations pending the time the Supreme Commander took over tactical command on the Continent. Bradley outlined his scheme with which the Field Marshal at once agreed. Plans were promptly worked out and orders issued. The ring of steel began to close around the trapped Seventh Army. After more than two months of stubborn, skillful resistance, Germany's still-powerful forces faced strangulation in the Falaise pocket.

It was not till hostilities ceased the following May and we began to flush the surviving members of the German High Command from their hiding places that the full story of the Battle of France could be written. Then details emerged, fitting pieces into the puzzle of German moves in Normandy.

Some of the revelations came earlier, of course, but we were too engrossed in pressing every ounce of offensive power against the Germans to have time for battle post-mortems till it was all over. We captured Major Lettau, the Germans' chief meteorologist, in the Normandy round-up, and he gave us one of the reasons why our forces had achieved tactical surprise on the beaches. From his own calculations, he estimated that June 4 was the last day we would attack in the current phase of tide and moon. If we didn't come by then, he had told the High Command, the invasion could be safely ruled out until the corresponding period in early July.

We thought the enemy was slow to react after the landings. The bombardment had thoroughly disrupted their communications. For long hours they were left in doubt of the exact nature of the attack which had struck with such overpowering force. With fragmentary reports from the beaches and incomplete information on the airborne landings, enemy Intelligence had difficulty sketching in the pattern of the attack itself. In addition, they couldn't be sure whether this was the full-out invasion, or part of it, or simply a raid in great force. As a result, it was evening of D-Day before the Germans took constructive measures to meet our penetrations of the Atlantic Wall. By that time, with almost no information of our landings at the base of the Cotentin Peninsula threatening Cherbourg, they moved local reserves to the eastern beaches where the British and Canadians were ashore.

Perhaps had the aggressive Field Marshal Rommel been on hand that day the reaction would have been swifter. Rommel, who was in charge of defending the Atlantic Wall, had boasted to Hitler that he didn't care where the invaders struck. From Holland to Lorient, his defenses were impregnable. But Rommel was far away from Normandy that morning of June 6. His Fuehrer had summoned him for a conference. Since the trip coincided with his wife's birthday, Rommel had stopped off at Stuttgart to pay her his respects.

On June 6, Hitler was holding his staff conference at the Klessheim, an old castle belonging to the Archbishop of Salzburg, where he had gone from Berchtesgaden to meet the new Hungarian prime minister. Although it had been the basic strategy of the Germans to shatter our invasion against the coastal defenses, the unpredictable Hitler had already discounted this barrier. He had lost none of his confidence. General Walther Warlimont, one of the youngest and soundest of the German staff planners, described Hitler's reaction for us. "Hitler's whole attitude," Warlimont recalled, "was that now the invasion had actually begun, all measures were being taken to meet the crisis. No, he did not believe it was possible to prevent the landings. But he believed that within six or eight days it was possible to throw the troops back into the sea. The German troops would emerge victorious through counterattacks."

Counterattack was what we most feared, too. It had

been our gravest worry during the planning days in England. The whittling down of the Luftwaffe, the bombing of the French railroads, the blasting of oil targets, had all been designed to hamper the Germans in reinforcing their Norman garrison. Now with the great undertaking actually on the Far Shore, we were straining every nerve and every resource to build up our strength fast enough to meet the massive German counterattack we expected. In spite of villainous weather, our troops and supplies poured through the sheltered anchorages and over the beaches. Work was pressed on the two artificial harbors. By D plus 9, the date on which we had estimated the Germans would be ready to counterattack, we could feel reasonably secure. We had half a million men and some eighty thousand vehicles in France. Our five beachheads, linked up all along the line, presented a solid front. But still the counterattack did not come.

We were correct in our estimate of the Germans' intentions. They meant to counterattack. Hitler, from Berchtesgaden, was demanding a plan from the tired Field Marshal von Rundstedt, Commander in Chief in the West. Rundstedt sent back word that the counterattack would be launched toward Bayeux to roll up each of the invading forces in turn till the entire expedition had been pushed into the sea. But Rundstedt was never able to put this plan into operation. He was still waiting on June 28, when Hitler impatiently replaced him by General von Kluge, for a sufficient striking force to mount his counterattack.

The reinforcements were coming. We watched the battle map at Supreme Headquarters as Intelligence identified successive German divisions entering the line. Most of the enemy armor in the West was on the way to the battle area, but the tanks were having trouble getting through. Our fighter-bombers rode the skies, diving on enemy convoys and concentrations of troops wherever they were caught on the move. In the face of this murderous opposition, the Germans traveled only at night, and the nights in June were agonizingly short for enemy armor and infantry on the roads. The Germans had optimistically planned to cover one hundred kilometers under screen of darkness. But with bridges down and rail centers blasted apart, progress was often cut to twenty. Convoys became separated; units appeared piecemeal in the battle area, often without their heavy equipment. However they appeared, they were thrown into the line. The High Command could not build up reserves for its counterattack. Their immediate need was too great.

After the early confusion had cleared and there was time to study our apparent intentions, the German generals saw two major threats. They decided that the eastern flank of our line, held by the British and Canadians, offered the greatest immediate danger because of the strategic terrain it faced. Col. Gen. Alfred Jodl, Chief of the Armed Forces Staff, also stated to us later that the High Command thought the British front was stronger than the American, the troops there more seasoned and aggressive. "This impression of ours remained unchanged," he confessed, "until the American attack on Cherbourg."

Cherbourg was the second of the two threats. The enemy must hold this town at all costs to keep us from getting the port. Risking the possibility that we might send a seaborne invasion against Brittany, the garrison there was weakened to rush infantry reinforcements up the Cotentin Peninsula where the Americans were proceeding with businesslike efficiency to cut the stubby neck of land in two. The Germans also tried to build a wall of troops across the base of the Cotentin to seal off our troops. But it was already too late. These were desperation measures, too little and too late.

Instead of developing a strategic plan with the broad objective of throwing out the invaders, the Germans were being forced by the speed of our build-up to plugging gaps in their line, rushing regiments and scraps of panzer units wherever the danger seemed greatest at the moment. What they needed most was more infantry. Without it, they were using armor to do the work of infantry in the line. To mount a decisive counterattack, they must hold the line with infantry and drive through with their tanks.

The German High Command tried to make up the deficiency by milking garrisons not only in Brittany but in southeast and southwest France. Still it was not enough. Divisions moved from Belgium to try the hazardous ferry crossing of the Seine, where they fell prey to our planes. There was not a bridge standing over the river below Paris.

The fatal mistake of the German High Command

during those weeks was to keep the strength of the Fifteenth Army alerted in the Pas de Calais area, while just across the Seine in Normandy the German Seventh Army was bleeding to death. The High Command found itself in a desperate dilemma. The generals were convinced that we intended to make another seaborne invasion somewhere along the northern coast. If the Fifteenth Army Forces in the Pas de Calais were withdrawn and a powerful invasion fleet appeared, Allied troops could walk ashore virtually unopposed. What was more, there was nothing to stop them from walking straight into Germany. It was a frightening prospect, and the Allied Command did everything in its power to keep this specter in the nightmares of the High Command.

Although we were well satisfied with progress in building up our forces, the presence of nineteen idle German infantry divisions on the coast of northern France and Belgium was a constant threat during those first perilous weeks on shore. It seemed incredible that we could persuade the enemy to hold them off when infantry was so desperately needed in Normandy.

Most of that June the weather fought on the side of the Axis. Our naval and transport forces accomplished heroic feats in the face of an almost continuous barrage from wind, sea, and sky. The cruelest blow fell on June 19 when a hurricane struck the coast without warning. There had not been such a storm in the Channel for forty years. The artificial harbor off St. Laurent, 90 per

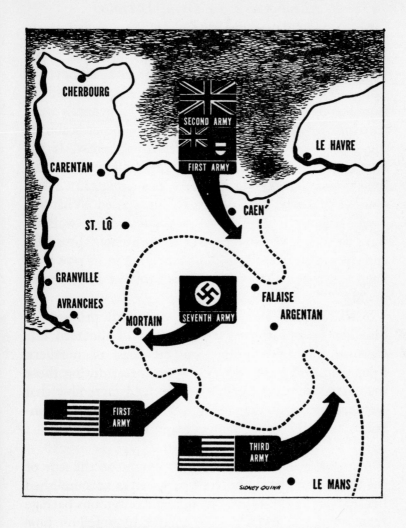

THE FINAL CAMPAIGN IN NORMANDY

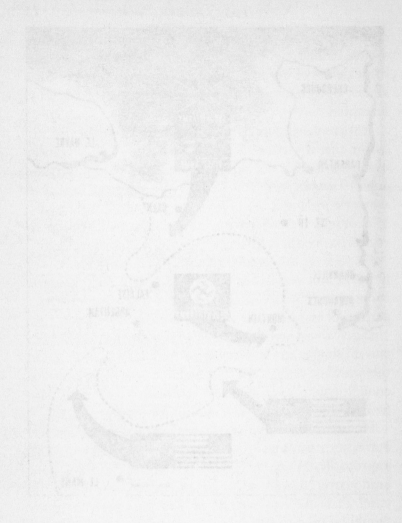

cent completed, disintegrated in the four-day blow which dashed eight hundred craft on the beaches and made debris of our installations along the shore. For days almost all communication with field commanders was interrupted.

It was sobering to recall, watching the violence of the storm, that if General Eisenhower had not made the decision to launch the invasion on June 6, this terrible June 19 would have come a few days after the next date when the tide met the conditions for our all-out assault. We should have been astride the Channel, unable to reinforce or support the troops already landed.

As soon as the storm blew out, General Eisenhower flew to France again for a conference with Field Marshal Montgomery and General Bradley. The character and pattern of the German defense had convinced him that changes were needed in the original tactical plan. He was no longer so much worried by counterattack as by the possibility that the Germans would move strong enough forces in front of us to create a stalemate. We needed elbow room badly—room to maneuver.

He was certain that the massing of opposition against our eastern flank made a breakout at that end of the line improbable. When he arrived at General Bradley's field headquarters on June 24, he had already made up his mind that the full weight of the American strength should be used to break out on the right. Field Marshal Montgomery had already arrived at the same conclusion. He had ordered the British forces to increase their pressure to hold the greatest part of the enemy opposite their

front. The eastern flank would become a pivot on which
the Americans wheeled and struck hard in the west.

But the offensive could not be launched immediately.
Cherbourg fell on June 26, midway between the maximum and minimum time General Bradley had estimated
for its capture—"Ten days if we're lucky. A month if
we're not." With its fall, the Americans turned south
for the agonizingly slow progress through the bocage
country where every small field was a fortress, every
hedgerow a German strongpoint. It was mid-July before
the troops emerged into the easier country beyond the
base of the peninsula where General Bradley could regroup his forces for the big push south.

Meanwhile, the Germans, nervously holding all along
the line against our pressure, had by no means given up
their plans for a major counterattack. The German hope
all through June was to withdraw armored divisions and
replace them with infantry then on its way to the front.
Two armored divisions were coming from Poland. The
new plan was that four or even six armored divisions
would rendezvous in the big forests southeast of St. Lô.
From there they would counterattack in a northeasterly
direction toward Bayeux and divide the American from
the British forces.

General Warlimont, the German planner, told us that
in mid-June Hitler discussed this plan with von Rundstedt and Rommel at a field headquarters just north of
Soissons. The attack never came off. The Germans could
not withdraw armor in the face of our growing strength.
"The infantry divisions did not arrive soon enough,"

Warlimont recalled sadly. "The armored divisions were still in the line, and even the two from Poland were committed in the line. By the time the infantry came up the armored divisions had taken such losses that their strength was no longer equal to the task."

By July 9, Lt. Gen. Sir Miles C. Dempsey's Second British Army had taken Caen after a gallant fight against strong resistance. The possibilities on our eastern flank were distinctly brighter. Now the Supreme Commander could see an all-out, coordinated attack by the entire Allied line which would at last put our forces in decisive motion. He set up a small advance headquarters in Normandy, not far from Field Marshal Montgomery. It was nothing but a forward base from which he could visit the headquarters of his commanders but it was free from the flying limitations of cross-Channel weather.

He was up and down the line like a football coach, exhorting everyone to aggressive action. He constantly urged his commanders to ask for full air support in their drives. He demanded strong pressure against the Germans at all times to keep the front in motion. We all felt then that our coming attack would force the Germans into the first of their withdrawals.

Field Marshal Montgomery's plan called for the Canadians to attack on July 17 to draw off enemy strength from the British front. On the following day, the British themselves would drive forward under full power. On July 19, while the Germans were occupied with the blow in the east, the Americans would strike south on the opposite side of the line. It was the boxer's "one-two" delivered in terrific strength. Each of these attacks would be preceded by the full weight of Allied air power in "carpet" bombing attacks, using fragmentation bombs to spread destruction among enemy troops without digging craters which would slow up our own advance.

The Canadian and British attacks got off on schedule but our old enemy, the weather, intervened to delay the American offensive. Although the infantry and tanks could have gone ahead, General Eisenhower and General Bradley were unwilling to start the attack until the skies cleared, so that the full weight of our air power could pin down the enemy at the jump-off and support the drive throughout. For six days the troops waited under dripping skies. Then, on July 25, the sun rode out once more. Tanks and infantry attacked in the wake of the planes.

On General Bradley's field desk that day was a letter from the Supreme Commander which expressed his confidence and hope for the great offensive:

Dear Brad [it ran]: My high hopes and best wishes ride with you in your attack today, which is the largest ground assault yet staged in this war by American troops exclusively. Speaking as the responsible American rather than the Allied commander, I assure you that the eyes of our whole country will be following your progress, and I take full personal responsibility for answering to them for the necessary price of victory. But a *breakthrough* at this juncture will minimize the total cost. General Montgomery's plan calls for a vigorous and continuing offensive by the other Allies in the line, thus allowing you to pursue every advantage with an ardor verging on recklessness and with all your troops without fear of major counteroffensive from the forces the enemy now has on this front. All these attacks are mutually supporting, and if Second Army should secure a breakthrough simultaneously with yours, the results will be incalculable. Good luck to every one of you.—IKE.

The advance was slow at first but it picked up during the day. By evening it was rolling. During the next few days, with the Germans attempting desperately to delay the forward columns by rushing reinforcements from Brittany, the drive gained momentum till by July 30 we had broken through at Avranches. Scattered debris of the defenders' demolished western flank lay along the route, and our line swept into Brittany. The breakthrough had come at last.

A new confidence and aggressiveness were apparent all along the line with the success of our attack. The Field Marshal sent General Eisenhower an enthusiastic message: "I have ordered Dempsey to throw all caution overboard, to take any risks he likes and to step on the gas for Vire!"

General Jodl was frank when we asked him to comment on the Normandy campaign a year later. "The landing as a whole was well executed," he judged somewhat pedantically, and then added with what appeared to be genuine enthusiasm, "but the Avranches breakthrough, if I may use the expression, was a piece of impertinence, and reminds me of Rommel's lightning capture of Cherbourg in 1940."

At Berchtesgaden, Hitler was talking counterattack

again, and General Warlimont was to visit the front as
the Fuehrer's personal observer to see how things were
going. Hitler discussed the possibility of withdrawing
into the interior of France but he warned Warlimont to
mention no such idea where von Kluge, who now had
the battle command, could get wind of it. "If von Kluge
questioned me about defense lines," Warlimont said, "I
was to reply that higher headquarters would take care of
building up any necessary lines in the rear to which the
Army might have to fall back. Hitler ended his instructions with the acid comment, 'Whenever a line of defense is built back of the front lines, my generals think
of nothing but going back to that line.' " This was on
July 31.

So the failure to plan a withdrawal was explained.
Hitler clung stubbornly to the notion that if such plans
were made, his generals would immediately act upon
them, and the aggressive spirit of the army would be
broken. Jodl knew how necessary they were but even
he dared not speak of withdrawal to Hitler. Commanders who mentioned the wisdom of constructing defenses
along the Seine, even after the Allied break-through,
were laughed at. Hitler was planning a counterattack.

At last the High Command had decided no second
invasion was coming against the Channel coast, and the
badly needed infantry divisions of the Fifteenth Army
were started across the Seine. The first moved out July
25, the day of the big American offensive. Others followed and went into the line before Caen. Finally the
tired panzers could be pulled out—but not for a rest.

This was the counterattack. Hitler ordered them to assemble in the hills around Mortain, northeast of Avranches.

On August 4, General Warlimont was hastily summoned from his inspection tour to General von Kluge's headquarters. Von Kluge was excited and disturbed. He had just received an order from Hitler to concentrate all the armor he could muster for a counterattack toward Avranches. He was to reach the sea and cut off American forces roaring south. But Hitler had also ordered him to restore a defense line with the German left wing close to Avranches.

Von Kluge was in a quandary. He was sure he could not restore the line and counterattack, too. Yet he realized how desperately the attack was needed. All the generals agreed with him, Warlimont said, possessed by the feeling that everything depended on a counterattack which would cut our communications at Avranches. They were convinced it would decide the issue in Normandy and the whole of France.

Hitler had hurried off to his headquarters at Rastenburg in East Prussia to deal with the growing weight of the Russian counteroffensive. There, poring over the Normandy battle maps, his intuition had a change of pace. He saw no need to hurry after all about launching the counterattack. Jodl transmitted the Fuehrer's order to hold off the operation until every plane and every armored car was in position.

Von Kluge, on the ground and with full knowledge of the desperate situation, knew that delay would be fatal. He told Warlimont that he dared not hold his attack beyond August 7. A spearhead of Patton's Third Army was already probing for Le Mans, where the Seventh Army had its principal supply depot. If von Kluge waited longer, he would be encircled. While Hitler, studying his maps, was reflecting blandly that the more Americans they let pass through the break at Avranches, the more they could isolate later and destroy, von Kluge jumped off.

It was already too late. Our ground troops resisted stubbornly, and for once the weather was on our side. Planes, RAF and American, strafed German panzers with rockets, blunting their force. Thrust after thrust was halted, but for five days von Kluge persisted before his broken forces were ordered to withdraw.

Warlimont saw the early attacks and went back to East Prussia, convinced of failure. "Hitler listened to me for almost an hour," he told us. "After I had tried to point out the striving by everybody to make it succeed, he only said, 'Von Kluge did that deliberately. He did it to show me that my orders were incapable of being performed!' "

On August 12, von Kluge was relieved by Field Marshal Walther von Model. When his plane arrived at Metz, the defeated commander was already dead by his own hand. Warlimont told us he left a letter to Hitler. He could not go on living, he had written, after losing his Fuehrer's trust.

Now, when the trap was already sprung, German armor and infantry tried to escape the jaws closing at

Falaise. The British and Canadians came south and west; the Americans drove east. The pocket became a killing ground. Still fighting with tenacity, the Germans strove mightily to save themselves. In spite of the great bag of prisoners, there was no such wholesale surrender as we had later across the Rhine. Tanks and Hitler's SS pets were given the first chance to escape. Infantry, which kept the gap open till the last, died where it fought.

When the Falaise pocket was finally eliminated on August 22, the great dividends of the Supreme Commander's decision were already flowing to us in the swift liberation of France. Field Marshal Montgomery's spearheads pushed to the lower Seine to spread destruction among the routed Germans at the river crossing. General Patton's flying columns had already reached the Seine above and below Paris. By August 25, one was across the Seine at Troyes.

The decision which brought these sweeping results was notable because of its hazard as well as its far-reaching objectives. General Patton's rapid advance had left a long unprotected flank to the south. There were effective German combat divisions in the southwest which might well be brought up to harass him. But there is an intuitive assurance which comes with major success. It must have infused General Patton during a conversation with Lt. Gen. Wade H. Haislip, one of his corps commanders. General Haislip was concerned about his thirty miles of open flank and pointed out that there were some sixty thousand Germans on his right who might very easily threaten his security. General Patton considered this situation for a moment, and then a twinkle came into his eye. "I'll tell you what you do, Ham," he said with gravity. "Just ignore 'em!"

During the lightning campaign across France, the air arm rode on our flanks. Allied planes were the eyes of the commanders, spotting concentrations of enemy troops, attacking them, and reporting their whereabouts to swiftly advancing headquarters. It was the first time in history that armies have left protection of their flanks to the air.

But a hazard greater than the now thoroughly routed Germans was troubling us—supply. It is no great matter to change tactical plans in a hurry and send troops off in new directions. But adjusting supply plans to the altered tactical scheme is far more difficult. It involves relocating vast depots and stores of ammunition which must flow to the fighting troops in an uninterrupted stream. Our bombing of French rail centers, which had contributed so heavily to victory in Normandy, now returned to plague us. The railroads were practically unusable. We laid out two-lane, one-way motor routes across France over which the trucks roared day and night to keep the advance supplied. Even this was not fast enough for the racing armored spearheads. They got their supply almost entirely by air.

Ports were the core of our problem. It was weeks before the destruction caused by German demolitions at Cherbourg could be repaired. Through all our drive eastward, most of the supply continued to flow over the Normandy beaches and through this crippled port. Now a major change was made in our general plan of supply. Enemy garrisons still held the Brittany ports—Brest, St. Nazaire, Lorient. Reckoning on the destruction they would cause before they surrendered, General Eisenhower decided to abandon entirely the project of using Brittany as a base.

Instead of a slow advance across France on which the original plans had been made, our troops were already in Belgium. Antwerp had fallen into our hands intact, when the British advance caught its defenders without demolition charges in place. Though the port facilities could not be used until the German garrisons were cleared from the mouth of the Scheldt where they controlled the approaches, Antwerp was now to be our major port of supply.

During these August weeks, I was supervising the movement of the tactical echelon of Supreme Headquarters from Portsmouth across the Channel to Granville. General Eisenhower was about to take command of the forces in person. On September 1, when Allied units were on the frontier of Germany, the Supreme Commander took over personal direction of operations. Night and day, in our camp under the pine trees at Granville, we drew the new directives to govern next moves against the Germans now behind the defenses of the Siegfried Line.

Our spectacular advance was slowing down, and transfusions were not enough. By August, pipelines under the Channel began to pour the tons of gasoline demanded by our swift movement. Sweating crews strung them along the highways across France. But it was impossible in the end to maintain our momentum. Shortages were developing everywhere. At Supreme Headquarters, with General Eisenhower impatient to give the Germans no time to rest and reorganize, we reached the reluctant certainty that delay was imperative to future success. The advance would simply have to wait until supply caught up. Antwerp was now the key to the situation.

We had won a colossal victory already. General Eisenhower's quick decision to seize the opportunity offered by the Germans had destroyed all resistance in northwest France. In two weeks our spearheads had raced from Normandy to the Siegfried Line. The invasion of southern France by General Devers' forces on August 15 made such rapid progress up the Rhone Valley that by mid-September our forces were linked from the Channel to the Mediterranean. Hopelessly outflanked, the remaining German forces in France gave up. Only a few of the ports remained in enemy hands.

Hitler's interference in the Normandy operations unquestionably played a considerable part in our success. The German generals sourly said so. Evidence backs them up. But it became a habit of German generals to blame every disaster on Hitler. The failure of the professional German military leaders to estimate and appreciate the weight and fighting quality of the Allied forces was certainly an equally decisive cause of their defeat.

Perhaps the ease of existence in France during four years of occupation had put softness in them and engendered a false sense of invincibility, born of their worship of German efficiency.

Certainly they had not counted on the speed of our build-up in Normandy. All their plans of grand maneuver to drive us out were frustrated by the increasing mass of divisions they found pressing against them. Although they held during the six weeks we needed to gain our break-through, it was my impression that none of the generals were prepared for the drive and skill of our maneuvers.

The simple fact is that the Allies outplayed the German field commanders and the German General Staff at their own game. Von Rundstedt, Model, von Kluge, with their horde of monocled, arrogant assistants, and the masses they led, were crushed, broken, and hurled back within the borders of Germany, and all western Europe, except western Holland, was free.

What is more, the Germans' shortcomings in France were noted down in the books of Allied planners and field commanders. They provided valuable lessons to Supreme Headquarters which contributed later to the destruction of the last reserves of military power in Germany.

SITUATION REPORT

* * * * *

FOLLOWING the victory in the Falaise Gap, our armies streamed eastward in three drives. Canadians of the 21st Army Group on the left swept across the Channel coast, overrunning many of the flying-bomb sites, capturing the smaller ports and a few of the larger, including, on September 12, the valuable prize of Le Havre. The advance was so rapid that Antwerp was surprised and taken on September 4 by the British 11th Armored Division. So swiftly had it come that the Germans had not prepared the demolition charges which could easily have hampered the use of the port. The airborne operation in Holland which was launched on September 17 failed of its full objective but was valuable in establishing a protective line above Antwerp. The British and Canadians launched drives to clear the German garrisons from the outer defense lines of the Scheldt River approach to Antwerp, and in late November the Allies were finally able to begin using that great port. The first ships were unloaded there on November 26. The

Germans had added the V-2 rocket weapon to their flying bomb, and these destructive killers, descending from the stratosphere without warning, caused great damage within the city, though their erratic direction kept most of them, purely by chance, out of the port itself. We advanced to the Maas in its entire length in Holland. First Army troops entered the Trier region in Germany on September 11 and in the Aachen area next day. On October 2, the First Army launched an attack through the Siegfried Line and, in the first two days, had breached the Westwall. Surrender of Aachen, the first important German city to fall, took place on October 21. The Third Army took Nancy on September 15, but it was not until November 22 that General Patton's forces conquered the stronghold of Metz. Meanwhile, the Seventh Army in the south was driving through the High Vosges across the Moselle and against the Belfort Gap area. Everywhere the front was kept in motion, though full power still waited on supply. The Ninth Army was waiting to cross the Roer River, held up by the Germans' threat of opening the dams and flooding out the countryside in the Roer Valley. The Third Army had begun an offensive against the Saar. The Moselle was crossed, and the Third Army was over the German frontier in a number of places. The weather was miserable. SHAEF Main was now established in Versailles where it would remain till March 1 when it was moved to Reims. The Supreme Commander had already set up an advanced headquarters a few miles from Reims which continued to be his personal headquarters until the end of hostilities. General Bradley was at Luxembourg; General Patton at Nancy; General Hodges, who commanded the First Army, was at Liége. Four thrusts proceeded simultaneously—Montgomery's on the north, Hodges' and Patton's (separately) in the center, and Devers' in the south. Their mission was to destroy German forces by attack and attrition, and start moving up to the Rhine. Allied supply difficulties had permitted the Germans to reinforce the Siegfried line, and now we would have to penetrate these defenses in force. We were doing it. All along the line the Allied troops were breaching the line, driving into Germany. But still we had two major objectives in the strategic plan. One was to mass supply in the north for the crossing of the Rhine to encircle the Ruhr. The other was to destroy Germans west of the Rhine and move all our forces up to the river barrier to take advantage of such opportunity for a crossing as might be offered. Then our plans were temporarily interrupted by the great German counteroffensive through the Ardennes—the Battle of the Bulge.

3. The Ardennes Counteroffensive

ON THE morning of Saturday, December 16, 1944, Lt. Gen. Omar N. Bradley, who commanded the American 12th Army Group, drove up from his headquarters at Luxembourg for a conference with General Eisenhower in Versailles. For the past week it had been quite clear to Supreme Headquarters that the Germans were up to something. The Sixth SS Panzer Army had crossed to our side of the Rhine and was suspected to be concentrating in the Cologne area, though its units were now maintaining radio silence.

The Fifth Panzer Army, which had been fighting us bitterly in the Aachen sector, was disengaging itself from the line. Whole divisions were withdrawing, and while this might be simply for the purpose of refitting and replacement—the units had been considerably battered—still the intentions of so much uncommitted armor were cause for the greatest vigilance. Further south in the Saar area there had been withdrawals of armor, too.

In addition to the panzers, whose recent whereabouts was at least fairly well known, we had lost track of several of the new Volksgrenadier infantry divisions. A movement of unidentified troops through the Eifel region behind the Ardennes had been reported by air reconnaissance. The Eifel-Ardennes was a quiet sector, except for the constant clashes of patrols sent out by each army, but these last few nights, our patrols reported, no Germans had been encountered. It was standard enemy practice to hold the area with three Volksgrenadier divisions, replacing them about once a month with others. Our Intelligence checked three new divisions into the line during the week but reported that the old ones had not come out.

These bits and pieces indicated almost certainly to Supreme Headquarters that the Germans were planning a counterattack somewhere. Studying the map and considering our troops' disposition as well as theirs, we had decided that the two most plausible areas would be Alsace, where our line was weak and sizable German forces chafed in a pocket around Colmar, and in the Ardennes.

The only logic that pointed to the Ardennes, in addition to the presence not far away of so much enemy armor, was that this was the most lightly held part of our entire front. We were taking a calculated risk in this area. Elsewhere along the line we were on the offensive. While our drives were limited for the time being, they represented important maneuvers to bring our troops into position for the push to the Rhine. Unless confronted by a definite and serious threat, to immobilize divisions for the purely static purpose of strengthening our defenses in the Ardennes would delay our offensive concentrations and final victory.

In itself, the Ardennes area contained no military objectives. The enemy's only long-range purpose in assaulting here could be to reach across the Meuse River, and the Meuse was fifty miles away. Any such objective would require a counteroffensive in great strength. A strong local counterattack, to be sure, would require us to move in reserves. It might temporarily slow operations on other parts of the front. But that same possibility existed in an attack anywhere along the line.

The Staff discounted the possibility of a serious counteroffensive, as this would require the enemy to employ all his reserves of men and supplies. The Germans would have to give up their present advantage of fighting behind the strong defenses of the Siegfried Line, so difficult for us to penetrate, and risk a crushing reverse which would make it impossible for them to defend the line of the Rhine. General Eisenhower, while accepting the logic of this view, was not convinced. He felt that the German High Command, goaded to desperation by defeat after defeat, might attempt a desperate gamble.

The Supreme Commander discussed the situation in detail with General Bradley and the Staff. Three American infantry divisions—the 4th, 28th, and 106th—were spread thin along the ninety miles of Ardennes front, with the 9th Armored Division backing them up. General Bradley was not worried. His estimate of the situation, first presented to the Supreme Commander many days prior to the attack, proved in the event to be almost miraculously correct.

Considering the tortuous terrain, he had believed for some time that in the event of a local enemy counterattack the American troops in the line, supported by several forward reserve divisions immediately available, could take care of any risk the Germans might be willing to assume. While they might secure a temporary breakthrough if they were willing to pay the price in precious reserves, it seemed improbable that an attack through the Ardennes could develop any broad importance in the general military situation along the entire front. At the very least, Bradley estimated, the Germans could be stopped on the Meuse, and east of that line he located no important supply installation.

We were discussing these possibilities in General Eisenhower's office when the first report came through. The Germans had attacked in some strength at the border of the Ardennes. The news was meager, as it always is before an enemy's intentions are fully disclosed. Tanks had appeared in several places, but this was not significant, as German infantry divisions usually had some tanks. Without waiting for details, however, General Eisenhower decided to back his own judgment. He acted instantly and with the greatest vigor. This was no local counterattack, he decided, thinking of the unemployed panzer armies. Power would be needed.

As events later proved when the enemy's plan was fully learned, the orders which the Supreme Commander issued in this emergency and the correctness of his estimate constituted the third of six great decisions that insured the defeat of Hitler's armies in the West.

General Bradley was directed to move the 10th Armored Division from the south and the 7th Armored Division down from the north along the flanks of the attack and to alert divisions on both sides of the Ardennes. At the same time General Eisenhower ordered the Supreme Headquarters reserve moved toward the zone of attack. The 82nd and 101st Airborne divisions were immediately available. They were reinforced by additional artillery, antitank guns, and transport, and directed toward Bastogne, at that time well to the rear of the existing front line. The importance of this town was apparent in the roads that crossed it on the map, and Bastogne was selected as a march objective for this reason. In spite of time required to reinforce the division, the 101st Airborne was at Bastogne in eighteen hours, beating its timetable by six hours at a time when minutes counted. The 82nd Airborne, meanwhile, was directed further north toward St. Vith, also a communications center.

With these precautionary moves made, we waited for more detailed reports. The weather was wretched. A cold blanket of fog hung over the Ardennes, masking the extent of the operations and making air observation or attack impossible. We surmised the Germans had counted on that. Since Normandy they had developed what Field Marshal von Model scornfully called "air neurosis," remembering what our fighter-bombers could do to moving columns and communications. General Bradley remained at our headquarters till next morning, while Intelligence sketched in the direction and size of the attack. By midnight of December 16, ten Volksgrenadier, five panzer, or panzergrenadier, divisions and one parachute division had been identified and located on the map.

A pattern was already emerging from the fog. The Germans had pushed three full armies into the Ardennes —the unemployed Sixth SS Panzer Army on the north toward St. Vith, the Fifth Panzer from the Aachen line in the center toward Marche, and the Seventh Army, a numeral risen from the ashes of its Normandy destruction, on the south toward Bastogne. General Eisenhower had been quite correct in judging that this was no local attack. The Germans were risking all their reserves in a full counteroffensive!

Field Marshal Montgomery in the north had also acted with great promptness. General Horrocks' British Corps of four divisions, bound toward its concentration area for attack, was halted and regrouped south of Antwerp, and 21st Army Group headquarters was providing for its commander the "tidiness" and tight control he demanded in battle. Allied offensive activity was halted in all other sectors to concentrate on this desperate attempt of the Germans to seize the initiative. General Patton was directed to turn part of his armor north toward Bastogne, already being attacked by the German spearhead.

To replace our general reserve sent into the line, the 11th Armored Division and 17th Airborne were brought over from England and moved to the Meuse. Other divisions crossed the Channel in advance of schedule to meet the possibilities of the new situation the Germans had created.

It is a pity that the most urgent military security prevented telling the story of the Ardennes as the battle unfolded. From newspapers I saw later, I gained the gloomy picture that the whole success of the Allied cause in Europe hung in the balance. General Eisenhower once said a little ruefully that he had never known we were in danger until he read about it in the papers. We were not unduly disturbed over the final outcome then or at any time. The German offensive moved far too slowly in its first days to gain important momentum. Enemy columns were advancing only about five to seven miles a day, whereas in our own great armored sweeps across France the tanks had often made advances of twenty-five to fifty miles in twenty-four hours.

The Germans could not have picked terrain less suited to their purpose. The array of armor was certain evidence that they looked upon this campaign as blitzkrieg. But blitzkrieg, which depends on lightning swiftness, was impossible in the Ardennes mud and snow. Heavy tanks broke the thin crust of frost and their treads churned roads into bottomless mire, blocking the impatient battalions behind. Detours over even softer ground were impossible. These conditions and the heroic resistance of our advanced divisions thwarted the German

drive during its first critical period. When the fog lifted
and our air power could be turned against both offensive
units struggling to advance and communications trying
to bring up supply, their defeat was certain.

Nevertheless, it was General Eisenhower's estimate of
the situation and the swift decision to rush reinforcements to flanking key points which robbed the enemy
of success. In this he was fully supported by General
Bradley, upon whose capable shoulders fell the responsibility for the early conduct of the land battle. Had the
Supreme Commander waited to judge the scale of the
attack before acting, our task would have been far more
costly in lives when the moment came for our own
counterattack.

If we had known then, as we learned later from members of the German High Command captured after the
close of hostilities, the precarious margin they had been
willing to accept in mounting this offensive, we should
have been even less concerned for the final result. By
evening of the first day—December 16—Col. Gen.
Alfred Jodl, Chief of Hitler's Armed Forces Staff, was
doubtful that the great Ardennes counteroffensive would
succeed. The German armor was not rolling according
to schedule, and everything depended on the panzers'
speed. A short thaw that came with the protecting fog
had made quagmires of the narrow dirt roads. In some
places, tanks were mired to their turrets.

In addition, the divisions of newly organized Volksgrenadiers had been unable to penetrate the strong

American resistance. Panzers were having to punch their own holes. Fighting through road blocks hastily organized by the Americans, the spearheads lost precious hours in what was to have been an all-out race toward the Meuse River bridges. By the end of the third day—December 18—it was soberly clear to even the most optimistic of the High Command in Berlin that their gigantic gamble for high stakes had but a single future—failure. They still hoped, however, that they could seriously impede resumption of the offensive by the Allied forces.

Through the delays caused by terrain and the fierce, skillful resistance of the Americans, the Germans had quickly lost the one advantage on which their entire enterprise depended—local surprise. Here, in outline, was their daring plan: Remembering how easily these things had been done in 1940, they intended to drive armored spearheads to the Meuse River bridges before we could organize opposition to stop them. Once the infantry had pierced our thin defense line, the tanks hoped to cut through without further serious resistance. Having crossed the river, the panzers would wheel and break for the Channel coast to seize the port of Antwerp and cut off our principal source of supplies. Antwerp was their objective. With this vital port in their hands, all the German forces in the West would concentrate on the powerful Allied armies divided and bypassed in the maneuver and destroy them in detail. That was the plan.

The German High Command had no illusion about the hazard of this bold undertaking. So taut was its timing that they knew it could succeed only if spearheads reached the Meuse by the end of the second day. That was why General Jodl and the others could recognize failure so quickly. They knew how fast our abundance of motor transport could deploy Allied troops to oppose them, once their intentions were clear. Their only hope was that surprise would get their spearheads through first.

A long time later, I had an opportunity to ask General Jodl why they had attempted the counteroffensive at all with such a slender chance of success. He shrugged his shoulders. "I fully agreed with Hitler that the Antwerp undertaking was an operation of the most extreme daring," he confessed. "But we were in a desperate situation, and the only way to save it was by a desperate decision. By remaining on the defense we could not expect to escape the evil fate hanging over us. By fighting, rather than waiting, we might save something."

To give the Ardennes counteroffensive its full perspective, it is necessary to sketch in briefly the situation all along the front. Our primary strategy, toward which all operations were pointed, was to cross the Rhine and get at the heart of Germany—the Ruhr. The main thrust across the river was to be made by Field Marshal Montgomery's forces, attacking toward the great North German plain. We also intended another crossing further south to reach into Germany through the Frankfurt corridor.

But before the big offensive could be mounted, General Eisenhower wanted the entire front moved closer to the Rhine. He felt that we must hold the west bank of the river at least as far south as Bonn and preferably along the entire front. He intended to reach the Cologne plain in the center and to push through the Siegfried Line further south. He was particularly determined to destroy the German garrisons in place, so that they would not be available later to defend the Rhine. In mid-November, limited offensives had been launched to achieve these objectives. Until we had a strong line for the general front, we could not spare the troops to mount all-out offensives at points of our own choosing.

The Supreme Commander insisted on constant aggressive action everywhere. Even the Ardennes sector had always been restless with patrol activity. Through an autumn of torrential rains and bottomless roads, we managed to keep the front stirred up all along the line and to inflict losses more than doubling our own. By mauling German divisions we could take a heavy toll of the enemy with far less cost to ourselves, because we were better prepared, clothed, and equipped for winter fighting.

The greatest urgency kept us on the offensive that fall and winter. The Germans were hastily organizing more divisions, and their program, as we interpreted it, would produce about sixty new divisions on our front by spring. If we could burn up these troops before they became battle-tried, the success of our last great effort was assured. During early December, when the front displayed no very spectacular activity, we estimated that the enemy was taking nine thousand serious casualties a day on the Siegfried Line, the equivalent of about five German divisions a week.

As General Jodl testified, they were in a desperate situation. We did not see then, and I do not see now in retrospect that there were any measures by which they could hope to do more than stave off disaster. They had long since lost the power to reverse the situation in Europe. Yet Hitler would not surrender. It was out of this mood of desperation that the Germans struck.

By December 19, when the counteroffensive was in its fourth day, we were already measuring how long it would be till we could apply the heavy pressure to the flanks of the lurching advance which would begin to strangle it. On that day, at a conference at Verdun, the Supreme Commander issued his orders to General Bradley, General Devers, whose 6th Army Group had been extended north in the emergency, and the air forces for initiating a full-scale counterattack by the Third Army against the southern flank.

Our greatest concern at this time was that we had overestimated the Germans' determination. We were afraid they might become discouraged too soon and order a withdrawal before we were in position to inflict maximum destruction. At a meeting on the morning of December 18, the Staff had expressed this anxiety to General Eisenhower. If the Germans could not drive in a salient deep enough to offer us the opportunity we now sought for a decisive counterattack, it might be

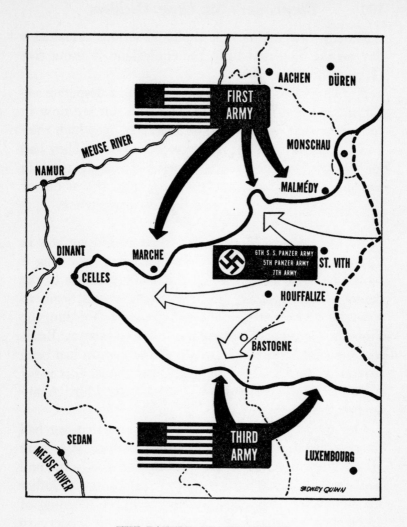

THE BATTLE OF THE BULGE

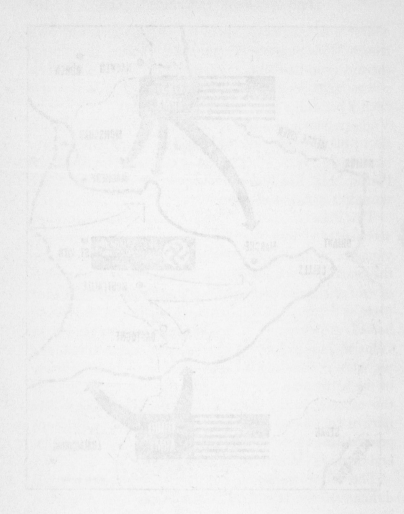

THE BATTLE OF THE BULGE

desirable to encourage them by pulling back our own troops. The Supreme Commander assured his officers there was no need for a "mousetrap." The advance was still moving, he pointed out, though at what must have been a painfully slow rate to the Germans. The reserve Volksgrenadier divisions in line were proof that this was an all-out offensive on the enemy's part. When I got back to my own office there was a call from General Patton. He had been wondering, too, whether we shouldn't bait a mousetrap.

This does not mean that the Ardennes break-through was regarded with anything less than the gravity and vigilance it demanded. Nothing is certain in war, and the situation was filled with hazard and tension. But none of us felt the anxiety expressed in an incident that took place at Supreme Headquarters in Versailles on December 18. A delegation of high French officers headed by General Juin had come up to discuss the situation, and we were conducting them to the war room for a study of the battle map. Ae we walked through the halls I saw the officers casting puzzled glances into offices where normal routine seemed to be going on. Then a French general behind me said to our Intelligence Chief, General Strong: "What! You're not packing?"

The salient driven into our line was so deep that it was difficult for the 12th Army Group from its headquarters in Luxembourg, on the south of the bulge, to supervise the American First Army to the north. General Bradley rightly estimated that there would be unfortunate psychological repercussions if his headquarters was moved back to a position from which he could effectively control both flanks of his armies. But Field Marshal Montgomery's tactical headquarters was conveniently located for control of the northern army. With Bradley's consent, Field Marshal Montgomery was charged with conducting the battle on the north flank of the salient while General Bradley directed operations on the south flank.

For several days, everything depended on the action of the 101st Airborne Division at Bastogne and on the 7th Armored and 106th Infantry Divisions in the critical area of St. Vith. These two rallying points were held by our troops with the utmost determination. Although the enemy battered his way into the town of St. Vith, the heroic garrison did not retire until ordered to do so when we had organized firmly the critical area of Monschau, the northern shoulder of the penetration. Securing this vital point resulted from the inspired work of the 2nd Infantry Division, supported by the 99th and later the 1st Infantry Division. The epic of Bastogne is too well known to need elaboration, but it is no exaggeration to say that the gallant 101st Airborne Division, as it held its ground against the attacks of a total of nine German divisions, meant to us the difference between success and failure of our countermeasures on the southern flank.

It was a formidable baptism of fire for two of the divisions holding the Ardennes. The 106th Infantry Division had landed at Le Havre only six days before and been trucked down to this quiet sector to gain experience. The 9th Armored had been in the vicinity since

October, but, except for patrol clashes, its tanks had seen no action. In spite of being bypassed in the penetrations, these divisions blunted the enemy's thrust and broke up the attacks during the first critical days. As it turned out, the 106th and part of the 9th Armored were in a vital area of the bulge. The Germans counted on the Sixth SS Panzer Army to roar through the northern sector and reach the river first. Resistance was so effective that the Fifth Panzer Army in the center actually became the point of the salient.

On December 22, the weather began to improve. Our air force rode out at last to begin its paralyzing attacks on armored columns and enemy communications. To protect his precious reserves, Hitler sent up the Luftwaffe in the strongest concentrations since we had been on the Continent. They struck at airfields and inflicted considerable damage in the savagery of their first attack. Our fighters whittled away at them. After one last big attack on New Year's Day, German planes were no longer a factor. So little did the German battle commanders think of their own air support that they reckoned the absence of the Luftwaffe as one of the principal causes of their failure.

Our fighter-bombers ranged in and out of the battle area, creating disaster among the enemy's road and rail movements. Now the struggling columns began to starve for fuel, food, and ammunition. On December 24, the counteroffensive reached its farthest penetration when a lone spearhead of the Second Panzer Division, lunging far beyond its support, dashed to within four miles of the Meuse. There, at Celles, progress halted ignominiously. As the tanks wheeled and made for cover, one complete armored battalion stalled and was captured. The tanks had run out of gas.

Next day was Christmas. The German High Command's present was an order to its troops to dig in and hold what they had gained. The Supreme Commander went to Field Marshal Montgomery's headquarters in the north to arrange for the necessary coordination between the planned counterthrusts from the two flanks. The Field Marshal was convinced that another heavy attack would be delivered against his wing and, since the perfect timing of his own attack would be on the heels of a defeated German effort, it was agreed that his attack would wait a few days seeking such a favorable moment.

On December 22, General Patton's forces had begun attacking north toward Bastogne. The day after Christmas, the tanks made firm contact with the defenders of that broken town. On the same day, Supreme Headquarters estimated that the enemy's drive was definitely at an end, even though additional minor attacks were to be expected to gain ground of local tactical value, if the enemy should hope to hold his positions.

On January 3, American First Army troops began counterattacking from the north toward Houffalize in the center of the bulge. Six days later, after the Germans had spent themselves at Bastogne, General Patton's forces resumed their progress to drive their southern wedge to Houffalize. Axis weather again intervened with heavy snow and ice. Many of our tanks entered action guided by a crew member walking in front to indicate the route. But by January 10, the gap between the converging pincers of the two American forces had narrowed to ten miles. Through this slim opening the enemy tried to choke the remnants of his broken forces, fighting fiercely against the closing ring.

It took six more days. Then, on January 16, a month to a day after the start of the offensive, the two American forces joined at Houffalize and turned their combined strength eastward in pursuit of three German armies. More than 120,000 serious casualties had already been paid by the Germans for their desperate gamble. They had lost 600 tanks and assault guns, 1600 planes. Even more important, their fuel reserves were spent. We had done decisive damage to their communications far behind the lines. Only disillusionment was the reward of the retreating German forces, towing fuelless vehicles when they could or abandoning them. The weary troops had given the best they had. They knew now it would never be enough.

The Ardennes counteroffensive was no spur-of-the-moment improvisation on the Nazis' part. They had been planning it in deepest secrecy for three months. Nor was it a conception of the generals. "The Fuehrer planned it all himself," Goering insisted when we asked him. "His alone was the plan and the idea."

Fittingly enough, it appears that the scheme occurred to Hitler while he was suffering from an attack of jaundice. The time was September, when his fleeing Western armies were taking refuge behind the Siegfried Line. The Germans had fretted over the urgency of some broad-scale countermeasure since their overwhelming failure in Normandy the previous month. General Jodl once pointed out, rather academically, that the ideal moment would have been late in August when our armored spearheads were racing through France so rapidly that they were also outrunning their supply. What made Jodl's judgment academic was that the Germans had no means then to mount a counterattack at all.

As we pressed the enemy into the Siegfried Line, the High Command was studying the possibility of a counterattack from somewhere along the German border. That was when jaundice put Hitler in bed. Jodl, who was a special favorite of his Fuehrer, paid him a call. Although Hitler disliked having anyone see him in bed except his aides, so Jodl told us, he received the General and disclosed his inspiration of a counteroffensive through the Ardennes to snatch at Antwerp.

Jodl sketched Hitler's idea on a map, showing the direction of the attack, its dimensions, and the forces they would need. Hitler wanted the base made wider to include a direct attack on Luxembourg. He was afraid that otherwise the advance would form a wedge and might be driven in from the sides in the first Allied counterattack. "Hitler's ideas were very sound," Jodl commented, though it seems probable that history will disagree. "It was my task," he went on, "simply to convert the idea into practical form, bearing in mind the troops we had at our disposal. Then a draft of the plan was made."

Hitler disclosed the ambitious scheme to Goering also, and a week later, when the Fuehrer was once more out of bed, there was a conference of Hitler, Jodl, and the Chiefs of Staff of Field Marshals von Rundstedt and von Model to get the planning started immediately. Von Rundstedt, who had been restored as commander in chief of the German Army in the West, would have over-all command. Von Model's army group would make the attack.

Soon after this first conference, Field Marshal von Model appeared at Hitler's headquarters with maps and a plan of attack. "There were slight differences between our ideas in the High Command and those of the front commanders," Jodl told us. "Model thought Antwerp too far to reach and beyond our means. He thought the troops around Aachen would be a danger to our advance unless they were wiped out first.

"Hitler and I believed we could not wipe out the very strong and well-armed Allied forces around Aachen," Jodl continued. "We thought our only chance was an operation of surprise which would cut the lifeline of the Allied forces at Aachen and in that way alone neutralize them. It was an act of desperation but we had to stake everything. The only chance of success was in a fluid advance over the Meuse."

Almost frantic measures were pursued to insure the secrecy of the coming operation. Everyone signed a paper, Jodl recalled, solemnly accepting the finality of court-martial if he revealed, through negligence or intent, any part of the plan. As new officials were taken into the secret, their names were zealously added to the list of the inner circle, and they signed the agreement. Precious reserves of fuel, vehicles, equipment, ammunition, and weapons began to be set aside and hoarded for the great moment. The male population was combed through for every man capable of firing a weapon to make up the new Volksgrenadier divisions.

Since secrecy made discussion of the plan by telephone impossible, Jodl journeyed up to Ziegenberg, near Giessen, where Field Marshal von Rundstedt had his command post, to confer on such details as the routes to be followed through the Ardennes, the amount of artillery preparation required, the extent of fuel and ammunition to be available to each unit. "Hitler went into all these matters intensely," Jodl explained.

In October, one of the most colorful of the conspirators was summoned to Hitler's headquarters, then at Rastenburg in East Prussia. This was Count Otto Skorzeny, an Austrian and a lieutenant colonel, tall, blond, daring—well decorated with dueling scars—who had the reputation of being Hitler's arch-saboteur. It was Skorzeny who led the detail of paratroopers that rescued Mussolini from his fortress prison following the Italian capitulation in September, 1943.

Skorzeny was to have a special and, indeed, the critical role in the Ardennes operation. Commanding a fast panzer brigade, he had been chosen to lead the lightning dash to the Meuse and hold the bridges until the main force caught up. In addition to this battle assignment, he was to organize and train a group of volunteers whose mission was to infiltrate the American lines in American uniform, riding captured American jeeps and tanks. Their job was to cut communications, misdirect reinforcements on the roads, commit acts of sabotage, and, in general, cause any confusion possible which would delay the Americans from organizing effective opposition.

Primary qualification for membership in Skorzeny's band was a good speaking knowledge of English. Some 600 men were sent him for intensive training. He picked 150 and organized them into small teams, each with a specific mission of reconnaissance, sabotage, or murder. But they were not trusted with the real secret of the Ardennes. Skorzeny told them an Allied offensive was coming further north and they were to infiltrate the lines.

On November 23, Hitler called his leaders to Berlin where the coming offensive was gone over in detail. Low rank at the conference was an army commander. The plan could hardly be kept from these high officers much longer, considering their mass of responsibility in the field. But to protect the vital element of surprise, they, too, were sworn to secrecy which barred them from discussing the operation with their key subordinates. Those outside the inner circle who had to be told something were given the Skorzeny story—an Allied offensive was expected, and the Germans were mounting a counterattack.

In timing the offensive, foul weather was the first requirement—to keep our planes from interfering. "I thought we put too much emphasis on bad weather," Goering protested. "It hindered us quite as much as it hindered you." November was judged the month worst for flying, and tentative dates were picked as the twenty-sixth or twenty-eighth. But when the time came, panzer and infantry divisions simply were not ready.

In the second week of December, the meteorologists promised four or five days of choking fog, which seemed ideal for the High Command's purpose. During the night of December 12, Hitler proceeded to Ziegenberg with his staff and guards to make the final decision at the command post. Two days later he gave the order to jump off on December 16.

At Ziegenberg Hitler held a meeting of his higher field commanders who would direct this gigantic gamble on which everything in the West depended. Army and corps commanders attended, but only a few of the division commanders were invited to learn the secret, even at this late day. Hitler made one of his typical harangues. He called on the spirit of Frederick the Great to fire them and recalled Frederick's triumph over the Austrians in the Battle of Leuthen, also launched through the mists of the morning. After he had finished, the generals formed a line and had the privilege of a personal word and a nod from their Fuehrer. The commander of the Sixth SS Panzer Army, Sepp Dietrich, who had the key force in the drive, tried to seize his opportunity to inform Hitler that his troops were by no means ready and urge that the undertaking be postponed. But he was swept along in the line. Hitler did not stay for the jump-off Saturday morning.

The Germans were thorough and even ingenious in the measures they took to hide their preparations from us. Holding the line that last night of December 15/16 were only the three Volksgrenadier divisions which we knew had just come up and the three that had not gone out. For six days no patrols were sent out from the German lines for fear prisoners would reveal rumors of activity far in the rear. They could not have disclosed the attack because the troops were never briefed. Company officers were told at last on the fifteenth, which undoubtedly accounts for some of the ineffectiveness of their men during the first important hours of the attack the following morning. The officers had no time to study maps and work out small-unit plans.

The panzer divisions were not in the line that night or behind it. To conceal their intentions, the Germans left them in their old positions until the last moment. Then they moved to the battle area under cover of darkness, at maximum speed and in radio silence. Many went straight through to combat without halting. The same procedure was followed with the infantry reserves. They did not move up to the rear of the assaulting Volksgrenadiers until after the first elements had jumped off. One panting division, brought down from Denmark, made the run to the front on bicycles.

The attack went poorly from the start. Instead of an easy break-through against tired or untried troops, the

Volksgrenadiers found the Americans resisting like fresh veterans. Skorzeny's brigade took its place behind the forward elements of the Sixth SS Panzer Army heading for St. Vith. The plan was that his unit would continue in this position until the column reached the Hohe Venn, a high, marshy plateau near the town of Verviers. By this time, the Germans expected to be well through the American line. Then Skorzeny would cut loose, make an end run with his tanks, and go straight for the Meuse. Paratroops had been dropped near Verviers during the night to break up any opposition which might be found and hold the area till he arrived.

But Skorzeny never came. The Sixth SS Panzer Army ran into bitter fighting long before it ever reached the Hohe Venn, and its advance became a traffic jam at St. Vith. By the end of the second day, Skorzeny knew he would not reach the Meuse. His only hope had been to dash across undefended country, avoiding combat, and now the area between his panzer brigade and the Meuse was swarming with advancing Americans. That was the end of Skorzeny's tanks.

Nor were his desperadoes in American uniforms much more successful, except in causing a great deal of anxiety to Allied Counterintelligence. A number of the small bands were captured almost immediately. From them we got the story, emphatically denied later by Skorzeny, that an important part of their mission was to assassinate General Eisenhower, Field Marshal Montgomery, and other high officers of the Allied Supreme Command. The story was too frequently repeated by isolated members of the band to be disbelieved. They said that picked individuals were to rendezvous on one of two nights in a Paris cafe. From there they would set out on their mission of murder.

It is true that a number of the masqueraders were picked up in Paris and that Counterintelligence got very little sleep for several nights. As for General Eisenhower, we regarded the threat with enough gravity to persuade him to remain in his headquarters, an unheard-of victory over his restless desire to go wherever trouble developed. Even so, he broke confinement to make a trip to Field Marshal Montgomery. At the end of four or five days there was no holding him. He rebelled and headed for the Ardennes.

In the entire course of the European campaign, this was the Germans' single attempt to seize the initiative. It is true that they obtained tactical surprise briefly at the outset, but that is not strange in war, particularly in the light of the extreme measures they took, which harmed as much as helped the power of their all-important initial assault. Infantrymen and tank crews went into battle fatigued by long marches. Fuel supplies which should have been adequate were dangerously low, and because of extended runs many of the tanks were in need of maintenance. But it was our air attacks on their tortured columns which the Germans felt decided the issue. General von Leuttwitz, commanding the Forty-seventh Panzer Corps, expressed the view of many senior German officers when he said after his capture, "In the Ardennes offensive the enemy air force, not having to expect German countermeasures, secured decisive success for the Allies. Against such air superiority, it would never have been possible, even with double the amount of divisions and the bravest troops, to accomplish this mission."

One principal element in the decisive German defeat was the battle leadership and staff work in Allied divisions, corps, and armies engaged. The performance of our commanders, ground and air, was of a very high order, and their men were beyond praise.

The Ardennes saw some of the bitterest, bloodiest fighting of the entire war in Europe. It called forth deeds of greatest heroism, and individual courage was routine. There in the snow and the mud, the American soldier proved himself invincible, and his resistance drained Germany dry of her precious reserves. Through all the remaining campaigns leading to the final surrender, the toll of the Ardennes was apparent in Germany's waning military power in the West. It weakened immediately the Nazi forces opposing us west of the Rhine.

Desperate though the gamble was, the German High Command saw it as their only hope. Actually they were attacking the morale of the Allied leaders as well as the Allied armies. If the fury of their powerful assault could stampede Supreme Headquarters into going over to the defensive all along the line and regrouping its forces, the Germans would gain precious time to build more defenses and comb out more men to delay the inevitable end.

If this was in their minds, they found no comfort in

General Eisenhower's Order of the Day, published to all the troops:

By rushing out from his fixed defenses the enemy may give us the chance to turn his great gamble into his worst defeat. So I call upon every man, of all the Allies, to rise now to new heights of courage, of resolution and of effort. Let everyone hold before him a single thought—to destroy the enemy on the ground, in the air, everywhere—to destroy him! United in this determination and with unshakable faith in the cause for which we fight, we will, with God's help, go forward to our greatest victory.

The date of the order is December 22, 1944, six days after the Germans first appeared through the morning mist.

SITUATION REPORT

* * * * *

By January 16, a month to a day from the beginning of the counteroffensive, the last smoke from German guns had disappeared from the Ardennes. The First and Third American armies had linked up at Houffalize, and the defeated Germans were in retreat toward the Rhine. At midnight of January 17, the First Army, which had been placed temporarily under Field Marshal Montgomery's operational command, reverted to General Bradley's 12th Army Group. The American Ninth Army, the Supreme Commander decided, would remain under Montgomery for the great northern assault across the Rhine. Field Marshal Montgomery wrote General Bradley a letter, telling him what a great honor it had been to command American troops and complimented him on how well they had performed in the Bulge.

Looking to the meeting with the Russians in the spring, General Eisenhower sent a message to the Combined Chiefs of Staff in December, asking permission to send a representative to Moscow to discuss the great

Eastern offensive by the Red Army and disclose the nature of our own operational plans. President Roosevelt, by personal message to Marshal Stalin, obtained his acceptance of a mission. Air Chief Marshal Tedder, General Eisenhower's deputy, took off for Moscow with the SHAEF G-3, General Bull, in early January.

On New Year's Day, the Germans unleashed a force of eight hundred planes against our airfields in Belgium and Holland, causing considerable damage. It was the Luftwaffe's last important sortie. Our own bombing efforts were against the synthetic oil plants in Germany to shrink supplies of gasoline and oil for planes, tanks, and motor transport. The German railroads were also systematically bombed, and Intelligence reported good effect against the railroads. At Hitler's direction, airplane plants—particularly plants working on jet aircraft —were being dispersed or put underground. The V-2 rockets still fell, with no means in our power to intercept them. But our capture of many of their launching sites had curtailed the number. The Supreme Commander now had eighty-five divisions at his disposal. Of these, thirty-five were allocated for the attack against the Ruhr in the north. The Malta conference of heads of state and military commanders took place in late January, precursor of the high-level conference in Yalta. The great Russian offensive—Stalin's four-pronged drive—began in January, but weather slowed it down.

In early January, G-3 reported that since June 6, Allied forces had taken 860,000 German prisoners of war. It estimated that in the same period the Germans had lost more than 400,000 in killed and long-term wounded. Plans for the great Rhine crossing in the north were perfected, and units moved into place. Landing craft, intended to ferry the troops, were moved up on great trailers. Artillery was put in position. All along the front there was movement as the operations in each sector were launched to bring the Allied force up to the Rhine. On March 15, before the northern crossing, General Eisenhower gave the first of the newly authorized Presidential Citations to a division—the 101st Airborne, which had performed so gallantly in its encircled position at Bastogne during the Battle of the Bulge. On March 1, the headquarters of SHAEF was moved to Reims, where the German surrender was to be made a little over two months later. The Red Army's offensive began to make headway. The Chief of the British Imperial General Staff worried about dispersal of forces in the campaigns west of the Rhine. Meanwhile, the Supreme Commander launched his series of planned attacks to kill off as many of Hitler's troops as possible before the northern Rhine crossing was attempted. With masses of Germans in effective organizations on the Rhine's western bank, he felt his crossing would be a hazard. His insistence was that they be eliminated before Montgomery jumped off.

4. Victory West of the Rhine

WHEN our rolling offensive across France reached the enemy frontier in September, 1944, two great barriers stood between the Allied armies and the heart of Germany. The first was the formidable defense system of obstacles, minefields, pillboxes, and strongpoints known as the Siegfried Line. The second was the Rhine. Between the two, though minor rivers remained to be crossed, there were no fixed defenses to slow our advance. With Teutonic singleness of mind, the enemy had put his reliance on one strongly fortified line.

It seemed to the Staff at Supreme Headquarters that when our guns flushed the German troops from their positions, correct enemy tactics would be to conduct successive withdrawals back to the Rhine, then retire beyond the river and blow the bridges. In this way, the Germans would take minimum casualties and husband their reserves. With strong forces along the broad water barrier, they could throw all their power into breaking up our crossings. Sound military judgment would not justify a determined stand by major enemy forces west of the Rhine once our armies were well through the Siegfried Line.

On the other hand, it was true that Hitler had ordered his forces in Normandy to hold their ground till they were past rescue by any means, and this stubborn stand had given us an opportunity to encircle and destroy the bulk of the German armies in France. They had done it once and they might do it again. The more he considered the situation in the light of the High Command's strategy in France, the more General Eisenhower was convinced that the Germans' apparent reluctance to withdraw from any ground they held might again be turned to our advantage. By adopting a bold scheme of maneuver, we might win a major victory west of the river.

We had long since planned to make our main Rhine crossing in the north above the Ruhr. To protect the flank of the crossing, it would be necessary in any case to clear the river for some distance south. Although this had at first been viewed as a simple defensive measure, the Supreme Commander had for some time seen the possibility of turning defense into an offensive strategy which would pay large dividends. His proposal was a series of interlocking campaigns to split up the German defenders and defeat them in detail. The Staff was directed to study operations stretching from Holland in the north to the Vosges in the south.

If we achieved the Supreme Commander's full objective, these battles would destroy most of the enemy troops west of the Rhine. Those who escaped across the river should be badly mauled and disheartened. The whole defense of the Rhine would be weakened. In addition to these advantages, with Allied armies against the Rhine along its entire length, the river would serve as our own barrier against German counterattack. We could mass our forces for additional crossings where we chose, leaving the line lightly held elsewhere.

On the basis of the Staff study, the Supreme Commander made his decision. Instead of a holding operation along the rest of the front while the main Rhine crossing in the north was being developed, we would embark on successive coordinated offensives. We would clear out the enemy as far down as the Moselle first, using this river as a strong southern flank. With that achieved, the power crossing north of the Ruhr could proceed without danger of interruption. The remaining offensives would then explode south of the Moselle till the entire west bank was clear.

Because of its determining effect on the remaining battles in the heart of Germany, this plan to fight a conclusive battle west of the Rhine became the fourth of the Supreme Commander's six great decisions which sealed the defeat of Hitler in the West.

The Staff of a high headquarters is always working several moves in advance, and these operations were planned in the early autumn of 1944. At that time we had moved to Versailles, where a staff conference was held early each morning in my office. Regulars in attendance were the Intelligence and Operations chiefs, Maj. Gen. K. W. D. Strong and Maj. Gen. H. R. Bull, G-2 and G-3 respectively, of Supreme Headquarters Staff. My Deputy Chiefs of Staff, Lt. Gen. Sir Frederick E. Morgan and Lt. Gen. Sir Humfrey M. Gale, Air Marshal Robb, Chief of the Air Staff, and Maj. Gen. J. F. M. Whiteley, our head planner and deputy G-3, were always there, as was a representative of the naval staff. Air Chief Marshal Sir Arthur W. Tedder, the Deputy Supreme Commander, and General Spaatz usually attended, and other officers were called in whenever some phase of the operation we were planning at the moment required their advice.

But we kept the meetings as small as possible. There was always coffee, and we usually found our most comfortable working position on the floor, with maps spread out. In this fashion, using as pointer the sword of the German commander of Versailles, who was captured when we took the Paris area, we plotted the further destruction of Germany's military power. As ideas were formed, we took the results to General Eisenhower's office for his decision. The campaigns west of the Rhine grew out of innumerable conferences of this sort.

Preliminary operations got under way in mid-November but for more than a month they were interrupted by the great counteroffensive which the Germans pushed into the Ardennes on December 16, 1944. The plans were little affected by the attack. In fact, the destruction suffered by the Germans from their disastrous attempt to seize the initiative made the possibilities even more promising. A good many of the reserves we expected to meet in the Siegfried Line were already destroyed.

Cologne. In view of the Germans' fondness for holding a fixed position, we believed they would fight savagely for the city and its industrial area. Instead of taking the casualties involved in a decisive battle at this point, our plan was to seal off the area with five American divisions, while the offensive broke out again below the city. Other elements of the First Army would attack from Euskirchen, twenty miles southeast of Cologne, toward the Rhine, while the Third Army drove through the Siegfried Line in a northeasterly direction. Through these converging offensives, the two armies would clear out all enemy forces as far south as the Moselle River.

The third phase of the battle would then be launched by the Third Army and General Devers' southern group of armies, planned again as two converging offensives, driving southeast and northeast toward the Rhine. When this was completed, we should have cleared the west bank along the entire length of the river, save for a bridgehead the enemy might retain at Cologne. If no opportunities had appeared for subsidiary crossings by this time, we could now mass our armies to force one, with the river as a barrier against German attack in other sectors where we did not intend to assault.

A strong sense of optimism was mixed with tension at Supreme Headquarters as the first of these operations began, and this feeling was shared by all commanders. Although the weather was still working for the Axis when February opened—a thaw had melted the thick snows of January, turning rivers into torrents and fields into lakes—spring was on the way. With clear skies our air

force would furnish the overwhelming margin of superiority to turn any attack in our favor.

We knew, too, from his shuffling of enemy divisions
and parts of divisions that Hitler was approaching the
twilight of his military power. Instead of the tough, well-
trained soldiers who made up his armies in the beginning, he was scraping the manpower barrel. One after
another of the commanders we captured in the Ardennes
told us that poorly trained troops slowed their assault.
German towns were now being protected by Volkssturm units, organized from local manpower into defense
brigades.

But while lack of training often reduced the skill of
German resistance in the later months of the war, the
tenacity of the German soldier remained his outstanding
characteristic to the end. So long as he was *facing* his
enemy, there were only rare instances when he showed
any tendency to surrender. He fought to the exhaustion
of his ammunition and often longer. The masses of
prisoners we took in some of our round-ups—in Tunisia
at the end of the North African campaign, for example,
in the Saar and Ruhr in March and April, 1945, and in
the closing operations throughout Germany—should
not be misinterpreted as evidence that the German was
a poor type of soldier with a weak fighting spirit. German soldiers surrendered in great numbers only when
our attacks broke through their ranks and we were
behind them. Then, when they were convinced the
situation was hopeless, when their higher commanders—
of divisions, corps, and armies—had either run away or

given themselves up, the soldiers themselves surrendered.

A number of garrisons like those at St. Nazaire and Dunkirk, although completely cut off, held out till the end of the war. Our long siege of Brest confirmed the tenacity with which the German soldier faced his enemy, as did our efforts to break out of the Normandy bridgehead during the early days of July. In the Siegfried Line, even Volkssturm troops fought with tenacity. Some of this quality was probably the result of dread engendered by the Gestapo and SS, which put fear in every German. The soldier in the line knew he was a hostage for his family at home. If he behaved badly by surrendering too soon, he could not tell what horrible fate might overtake his loved ones at the hands of Himmler's agents.

As for their general competence as soldiers, in spite of the reputation as supermen which the German troops gained in the days of their first blitzkrieg when the going was easy, we found them to possess only an average degree of professional and technical training, which did not measure up to the high standards of our own armies. In many cases, this was also true of higher commanders and staff. But the German soldier's tenacity made him a formidable enemy.

Hitler's acute manpower problem in these last days of winter was summed up for me by General Strong. "The enemy's capabilities grow fewer," his estimate read. "Today Hitler's only real ones are the measures he can take to stave off the day of unconditional surrender. By a flat refusal to admit defeat and by concentrating what remains of his resources on one front or the other, Hitler may be able to prolong the struggle, but he cannot overcome the irrefutable fact that each day Germany's position deteriorates in relation to the power of the Allies.

"The results of the Russian offensive have now disclosed that the Ardennes gamble pales into insignificance beside that which Hitler took in the East in order to be able to mount the Ardennes attacks. He is now suffering from the results of sending divisions belonging to the East to the West in November, only to be decimated until they no longer resemble divisions. Similarly he is suffering in the West by the absence of what remains of 6th SS Panzer Army and other divisions transferred to the East. Defeated in December and January in the West, torn asunder in the East and now again in the West, Hitler's juggling with divisions has been lamentable. His timings, which at first may have appeared to be sound, now show themselves to be entirely faulty. Time and the Allies wait for no man. Not even Hitler."

We asked Goering, after his capture at the end of hostilities, whether there had ever been any plan in the shuttling of divisions between the Eastern and Western fronts. He shook his head. "The troops were sent wherever there was a fire," he explained. "For instance, if the Eastern command wanted troops for an anticipated action and the West desired troops to check an attack already in progress, the troops were usually sent to the West. But it was the same principle as a fire department. Hitler, of course, made the final decisions."

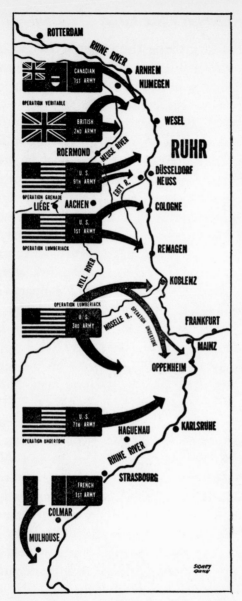

THE ATTACKS WEST OF THE RHINE

133

Operation VERITABLE, launched by the Canadians and British on February 8 and pursued to success with stubborn valor, became one of the most bitterly fought actions of the entire war in the West. We had planned to swing a swift, hard armored punch. But the thaw made such tactics impossible, and troops advanced across flooded roads and fields, sometimes waist deep in icy water. In spite of these difficulties and the enemy's fierce resistance, we got our foothold on the Rhine. By February 21, the Canadians and British were in position along the river. A pocket of German resistance remained on the west bank till March 10, where a body of the determined parachute troops held out opposite Xanten. Finally disheartened and outflanked by the advance of our Ninth Army, they withdrew across the river, blowing their bridge behind them.

The American Ninth Army's Operation GRENADE was originally timed for February 10, to coordinate with the Canadian and British VERITABLE. But the atrocious weather and flooded valley of the Roer River held our troops in check. The Germans were unable to blow all the dams before their capture but they opened enough sluices so that the river rose four feet. The crossing was too hazardous to attempt until the waters fell. It was February 23 when the assault boats pushed out from the muddy banks. After one counterattack on the eastern shore, the Germans fell back, and the Ninth Army rolled northeast. It picked up speed and prisoners. By March 2, Neuss was seized, and the troops stood on the Rhine.

In these actions and the ones that followed, the un-

even quality of the German troops was apparent everywhere. When the Canadians and British began their
offensive, they ran into skillful and violent resistance
from the veteran parachute army in the north. Some
German units died to a man rather than surrender. But
this eased the progress of the American Ninth Army,
since German troops had been moved from that front
earlier to meet the threat further north. After sharp resistance at first, the Americans found the Volksgrenadiers of the German Fifteenth Army accepting the hopelessness of their situation. Instead of dying, whole units
surrendered to a man. Resistance was as unpredictable
as that all along the line.

Although the urgency of future planning usually kept
me at Supreme Headquarters during this period, I took
time for a visit to the front at Neuss to talk with the
commanders and gauge the momentum of our offensive.
General Eisenhower was constantly appearing in the
forward lines and at München-Gladbach, after talking
with the troops, he remarked that they sensed victory
and were unstoppable. I had that feeling, too. General
Simpson, who commanded the Ninth Army, had an observation post in a large flour mill on the banks of the
Rhine at Neuss. I stood beside him in the tower watching our shells as they fell in Düsseldorf just across the
river.

It was a strange and incongruous sight, looking from
the town below to besieged Düsseldorf. At Neuss our
infantry and machine gunners occupied the front along
the river. Masses of our artillery were in position in the

outskirts of the town. Shells passed overhead with a steady roar to burst in Düsseldorf. Yet in the streets of Neuss, the population moved about in listless disregard of the danger. Men, women, and children seemed to feel they had endured the worst and nothing more mattered. I noticed a few babies in perambulators who took a brighter view, in spite of the incessant noise.

Among our troops there was an air of expectancy. At last they were going somewhere—fast. Pushing north, the Ninth Army made contact with the Canadians and British in the Geldern area, and the two fronts joined along the river. By March 5, between Neuss and Homberg, the Rhine was in our hands. Now, while the front blazed further south, our northern group of armies under Field Marshal Montgomery began to bring in the landing craft and line up the artillery for the all-out power crossing that pointed straight at the Ruhr. Their preparations were concealed within the fog of an almost constant smoke screen.

The tempo quickened as Operation LUMBERJACK, the second phase of these coordinated offensives west of the Rhine went into gear. In the first place, Cologne failed to hold out. Although resistance was stiff as the American First Army pursued its attack across the Erft River northeast of the city—fighter-bombers were summoned to break up opposition by strong enemy armor—for once the German High Command decided to abandon last-ditch resistance. The veteran troops defending Cologne withdrew across the Hohenzollern Bridge, leaving forlorn Volkssturm units to take the pounding of our artillery and deliver the unexpected prize into our hands. By evening of March 7, we were in full possession of what was left of Cologne.

The awe of desolation hung over this once great city when I entered it, not long after its capture. The center of the ancient town was completely flattened, a picture of absolute destruction greater than I had seen anywhere. Its death was mirrored in the lifelessness of living faces in the streets. Whatever these people felt once for the tawdry glamour of their Fuehrer, it was gone. Cologne was a preview of the fate which now hung precariously over all Germany.

Only the cathedral stood intact in the mass of rubble. I walked through it with Lt. Gen. J. Lawton Collins, who commanded the First Army's VII Corps, and we looked from the eastern windows across the Rhine. Before us was the broken structure of the magnificent bridge the Germans had blown on the heels of their retreat. It was this explosion, so one of the priests told us, which had damaged the handsome ceiling of the cathedral. Structurally, the building was still sound.

To the Staff, the capture of Cologne was like finding five new divisions. The units we had assigned to seal off the city were now free for other operations. But this was only the beginning of our good fortune. That same March 7, the 9th Armored Division to the southeast was clattering toward the Rhine, its objective the town of Remagen. As an armored spearhead came abreast of the hill overlooking the town, the Ludendorff railroad bridge still stood intact, carrying traffic east.

The 9th, like all other units, had been primed by General Eisenhower's instructions to seize any opportunity for a crossing. It seemed improbable that the bridge would be allowed to stand long enough for the troops to reach it, but a platoon raced down the hill and began battling its way through the town. At 3:15 a captured prisoner said the bridge was to be blown at four. At exactly ten minutes of four the first Americans reached the western end, and the bridge still stood.

At that same moment, the enemy set off the first demolition charge. It blew a crater in the flooring of the western approaches. The second explosion, touched off just as the Americans started across, knocked out one of the principal diagonal supports. The cap snapped on five hundred pounds of TNT, but the charge itself failed to explode. In the face of these direct warnings of imminent death, the Americans raced on. Our Engineers cut wires leading to charges beneath the deck and sped across to break the main cable controlling all demolitions, while infantry attacked the bewildered Germans. One group of defenders incomprehensibly retreated into the railroad tunnel. Flak batteries mounted on the steep slope above gave the principal resistance, which was savage until our men scaled the height and silenced the guns. Troops poured across, and the bridge was filled with running Americans. We were over the Rhine!

Battle requires many brands of courage, but the handful of infantrymen and Engineers who ran out on Ludendorff Bridge that afternoon performed one of the most daring acts of the war. They were seasoned to meet death along the roads and in the fields. But here, above the Rhine on a structure loaded with explosives, they faced the almost certain prospect of being blown into the river far below. The bravery of those few men had a decisive effect on the future fortunes of the war. As General Eisenhower said, the bridge at Remagen was "one of those rare and fleeting opportunities which occasionally occur in war and which, if grasped, have incalculable effects in determining future success."

General Bradley telephoned the news to the Supreme Commander, and back at Headquarters General Eisenhower grinned his pleasure. Exploit it, of course, he directed. Put at least five divisions across. The possibilities which the crossing opened were the break he had hoped for. From this point, we could pour troops into the Frankfurt corridor and stage our double envelopment of the Ruhr. The thing now was to hold the bridgehead.

Remagen was not in the area where we should have chosen to cross. The terrain behind it was rugged. There was little chance for open warfare on the forested plateau which leveled out behind the steep bank. Further inland, a north-south autobahn offered the first favorable ground for pressing into the interior. But there was no question about the value of our prize. The First Army rushed its build-up and braced for the counterattacks.

The Germans played into our hands. They allowed the local danger to blind their military judgment. Repeating the tactics which had brought them disaster in Normandy, they threw divisions piecemeal into the line.

A strong counterattack those first few days might have succeeded in driving out our bridgehead. Then we were too strong. Enemy planes buzzed the bridge angrily, trying to knock it out with bombs. Swimmers tried to destroy the supports with demolition charges. Our Engineers rushed supplementary bridges over the Rhine. On March 17, the center span of the Ludendorff, weakened by artillery fire, finally toppled into the river. By then we no longer cared. But for a time, the bridge had been worth its weight in gold.

The bridge brought about the final downfall of Field Marshal von Rundstedt as Commander in Chief in the West. He had been dismissed once in Normandy when his strategy bore no results. Later, he was restored to lead the luckless offensive in the Ardennes, where, in 1940, he had won his most spectacular success with the blitzkrieg which erupted into France by that very route. With our forces actually over the Rhine, von Rundstedt again went into eclipse. Field Marshal Albert Kesselring came from Italy on March 12 to pick up the flickering torch.

After he became a prisoner of war, Kesselring was still furious whenever he recalled the bridge. "Never was there more concentrated bad luck at one place then at Remagen," he fumed, when we asked him about it.

As Kesselring recounted the story, everything went wrong. In the first place, the bridge commandant was absent on that most crucial of days. A major of Engineers was in charge. We had thought he was at least stupid. Kesselring called him "a criminal." When at last he tried to blow the bridge, there was no time to fix the faulty wiring. "Of course, what should have been done —and what was actually ordered after the Remagen fiasco," Kesselring said, "was to install a radio-controlled igniter so that if the wires failed the charges could have been set off by radio." Four of the Germans considered most responsible for our success were court-martialed and shot. The Engineer major was lucky. We had picked him up at the tunnel, and he was safe as a prisoner of war.

Not all the Germans' blundering came at the bridge itself. Division and corps commanders, thrown into panic by the first American troops across the Rhine, began to move their headquarters instead of taking immediate aggressive action. Kesselring said these field commanders on whom everything depended were completely out of touch with higher authority. They could not be reached to take orders for the counterattack which they should have ordered themselves. As a result, although German troops were moved against the bridgehead in an almost patternless attempt at countermeasures, our build-up was faster than theirs.

Kesselring made no secret of the discouragement the bridgehead spread through the High Command. "The decisive importance of the operation at Ludendorff Bridge was clearly recognized everywhere," he said emphatically. "It disturbed the systematic build-up of the Rhine defenses. Troops meant for the defense of the Rhine area in general were frittered away at this point of break-through, which was in itself unimportant for the Rhine defenses as a whole."

Goering was even more downcast by the Remagen episode. "It made a long Rhine defense impossible," he admitted, "and upset our entire defense scheme along the river. The Rhine was badly protected between Mainz and Mannheim as a result of bringing reserves to the Remagen bridgehead." That may have had something to do with the lack of determined opposition when General Patton's troops forced a second crossing at Oppenheim further south. The reserves had been rushed to put out the fire at Remagen. "All this was very hard on Hitler," Goering observed sadly.

Hitler was also disheartened, so Goering said, by the spectacular progress of General Patton's troops a few days earlier. After seizing bridgeheads over the Sarre River, they had crashed through the Siegfried Line at Trier on March 2, clearing the area between the Saar and the Moselle. "We could not believe that these fortifications had been penetrated," Goering said. "That break-through and the capture of the Remagen bridge were two great catastrophes for the German cause."

There were more catastrophes in store. As the southern prong of Operation LUMBERJACK shook loose from resistance, Third Army tanks threw two spearheads to the Rhine—at Andernach and just above Coblenz. By March 11, the left bank of the Rhine had been cleared between these two points, and the destruction of the enemy north of the Moselle was practically complete. With the First Army busily preparing for a breakout from the bridgehead of Remagen and with the Third Army in possession of the objectives assigned its troops in Operation LUMBERJACK, the second phase of these campaigns west of the Rhine was finished. Our southern flank rested firmly on the Moselle.

The flying weather, after a bad start, began favoring us as the campaigns progressed, and we had all the power which air superiority provided. By now, the tactical co-ordination of air and ground forces had become an in-strument of precision timing. Again and again, ground commanders called with confidence for air assault to reduce troublesome opposition. At Remagen, our planes provided constant cover over the bridge, protecting it through critical days against persistent German attacks by single German bombers. Fighter-bombers, running interference for the tanks, added enormously to the speed of our spearheads. The Luftwaffe gave us very little trouble and no comfort at all to the battered Ger-man ground troops.

The wind-up campaigns in the south were set in mo-tion March 15 to finish the business of clearing the enemy west of the Rhine. Operation UNDERTONE fol-lowed the plan of the earlier offensives with coordinated attacks moving southeast and northeast to converge at the Rhine. The northern force was supplied by General Patton's Third Army. The southern arm was swung by General Devers' Army group, which had been greatly strengthened without the enemy's knowledge. The mo-mentum of the first day's attack carried the Seventh Army as far east as Hagenau.

Third Army troops further north had much harder going at first. At this point, estimating the situation, the Supreme Commander approved General Bradley's proposal to send another powerful spearhead of General Patton's tanks across the lower Moselle to drive into the enemy's rear. This attack caught the Germans completely by surprise. Following the direction of General Patton's earlier success north of the Moselle, enemy Intelligence expected these forces to continue across the Rhine at Remagen. They were totally unprepared for a lusty offensive at their back and collapsed in demoralized confusion when the armor cut through. Coblenz itself was occupied, and the river cleared down to the Mouse Tower at Bingen bend. By March 22, we had Mainz.

That night General Patton moved swiftly. Following the utter disintegration of the Saar defenses, the enemy had dragged broken remnants across the Rhine and blown the bridges. But the Germans were in no condition to defend their barrier, and we went through the gate with the crowd. Under cover of darkness, the American 5th Infantry Division launched a bold surprise crossing in small assault boats against only feeble resistance. Two nights later, on March 24, we had a bridgehead on the east bank nine miles long and six miles deep. From this new springboard our troops jumped the Rhine in force to seize Darmstadt and advance on Frankfurt, where they would meet the First Army erupting from the Remagen bridgehead into the Frankfurt corridor. By March 25, when our troops in the north were

already over the Rhine in force, all resistance west of the river had ceased. As March went out, we had six more bridgeheads in the south, and the Rhine was no longer a barrier. It was our river. Allied ships patrolled its waters, commanded by a Royal Navy commodore we called "the admiral of the Rhine."

To a staff officer in a high headquarters, the satisfaction of battle is in the results that flow from careful planning. No results could have been more spectacular than those which followed the flexible plans for the campaigns west of the Rhine. General Eisenhower's belief that the Germans would choose the fatal course of fighting till it was too late to withdraw proved correct in every instance except one. At Cologne the enemy retreated across the river with forces intact.

A shrewd commander profits by his enemy's mistakes, studying his tactics and strategy in detail. As a boxer sizes up his opponent's style of fighting, hunting out his weak points and his strength, a high commander learns the pattern of the enemy's strategic thinking and turns it to his own advantage. That is why the names of important planners are concealed whenever possible. Since they assist the commander by preparing his plans, to identify them would give an adversary valuable clues to the type of operation he might expect. For example, both Kesselring and Jodl told us they came to identify the Americans with bold, dashing maneuver after the Avranches break-through in Normandy. Unfortunately for the Germans, however, any advantage this estimate might have brought them was neutralized later on by

their lack of means and mobility. They were dead sure we intended to close the Ruhr by double envelopment. But they were powerless to prevent it.

The smooth execution of successful operations may leave the deceptive impression that the problem was not as difficult as it had seemed in the planning stage. The fact is, unless plans are developed to provide for every contingency that may arise, success is jeopardized. The campaigns west of the Rhine were enormously complex operations. Results of the offensives in the central and southern zones could not be fully gauged in advance. Their outcome depended too much on the reaction of the enemy. We had to be prepared so thoroughly that troops and supplies could be rerouted at a moment's notice to take advantage of such a break as occurred at Remagen. When we took the bridge, administrative plans of three army corps had to be redrawn immediately to get these troops into the bridgehead with their mass of guns, vehicles, and supply.

General Eisenhower's decision to defeat the enemy west of the Rhine robbed the Germans of reserves that would be desperately needed to defend the homeland. Instead of recognizing the disastrous result of trying to stand in place, the enemy held till defense positions were cut through and it was too late to save the demoralized troops. Once more the German High Command had tried to plug the line everywhere. By following this strategy of desperate opportunism, they now could plug it nowhere.

As for the Staff at Supreme Headquarters, transferred

since March 1 from Versailles to Reims, there was no pause with the end of these campaigns. Allied troops were already closing powerful pincers around the Ruhr. We were planning the final offensives which would complete the destruction of German forces driven back into their shattered fortress beyond the Rhine.

SITUATION REPORT

★ ★ ★ ★ ★

THE STAGE was set now all along the front of the vast European theater of war. The final act to bring about destruction of enemy forces was to begin on March 23 with the massive northern crossing of the Rhine. The First Army, with three full corps, was poised in the Remagen bridgehead, ready to surprise the Germans by breaking out toward the south, rather than to push north along the Rhine's east bank as the enemy had expected. An enemy force was being hastily assembled to create a line across the Sieg River, but Bradley had no intention of going that way. In a last desperate offensive attempt, there was increased U-boat activity against shipping in the Channel and in the North Sea. Back in Brittany, the stubborn German forces at St. Nazaire and Lorient still held out in meaningless resistance, contained by the American 60th Infantry Division. The Allies were content to let them stay. The V-2 and flying-bomb launching sites had long since been silenced in northwest France and along the Channel. Holland was now the only conquered territory from which these missiles could still be launched. The Russian advance through East Poland had been slowed by the thawing earth of late winter. Tanks were confined to the roads. But when the Red Army reached western Poland and eastern Germany, the roads were better, and the advance picked up momentum as it rolled toward the Oder River. SHAEF was worried about the German production of jet aircraft. The enemy was rumored to have produced as many as eight hundred in the hidden, underground factories, beyond reach of our bombers. Working under top priority, German mechanics, so the reports went, were finishing two hundred of these new craft a month. Some appeared in the sky, but never in force. We had no operational Allied jets in Europe. A Canadian corps from Italy and a British division from the Middle East were brought in at Marseilles and passed through the American lines to join Field Marshal Montgomery's 21st Army Group. SHAEF had moved to Reims, but the Supreme Commander made frequent visits to the battlefields during the course of the campaigns which brought us up to the Rhine. On March 6, General Bradley motored to Reims to talk over future developments with General Eisenhower, and waited over a day to lunch with Prime Minister Churchill. Mr. Churchill had been at the American Ninth Army's front and was enthusiastic over the advances made. That evening when General Bradley returned to his headquarters at Namur in Belgium, he soon had triumphant news to phone back to the Supreme Commander. General Hodges had called him. That was the afternoon when the Ninth Armored Division seized the great Ludendorff Bridge at Remagen, and American troops were across the Rhine. The Germans began their last desperation moves. They were directing their principal remaining forces toward the defense of the Ruhr opposite Montgomery, but they faltered in this purpose to divert badly needed divisions against the Remagen bridgehead. This, in turn, weakened the strength that was to be available two weeks later to oppose our forces in their push to the cities of the Ruhr. Nor could the Germans find enough offensive strength to stop the build-up of American divisions east of the Rhine in the bridgehead. By March 17, the day the great span fell into the river, the enemy had mustered but twenty thousand troops against this vital threat. They were not enough. Now as the climactic day of March 23 approached, bombers flew continuous sorties to the airfields from which jet planes might be launched. The extra-long runways required by jet aircraft were cratered so they could not be used; planes were destroyed on the ground wherever they could be found. General Eisenhower was on the Ninth Army front that evening of March 23, watching the artillery bombardment which began at eight o'clock, walking and talking with the men as they marched down to board the landing craft which would carry them across the Rhine in the night. At nine o'clock the artillery barrage lifted, and the British 1st Commando Brigade pushed off from the west bank, pointed toward Wesel on the far shore. The final phase of the war in Europe had begun.

5. Encirclement of the Ruhr

OPERATION PLUNDER, the last great Allied offensive of the war in Europe, began with a massive artillery bombardment on the evening of March 23, 1945. Its immediate objective was to send two armies, one British and one American, crashing across the Rhine north of the Ruhr. Once on the east bank, they would consolidate quickly and push forward in a sweeping arc to encircle the industrial heart of Germany. For more than two weeks the tremendous preparations between Rees on the north and Rheinberg some twenty miles to the south had been concealed from enemy observation in a swirling blanket of chemical smoke. Within this artificial mist, the artillery had been placed in position and troops grouped for the assault. Landing craft had been trucked overland to serve as ferries. Operation PLUNDER was being staged as a full-scale amphibious offensive, the greatest since the Allies went ashore in Normandy.

Across the Rhine, the whole of Hitler's Army Group B, commanded by Field Marshal Walther von Model, was deployed in mobile defense. Until the crossings began, there was little the Germans could do to hinder preparations or to break up the gigantic assault they knew was coming. Von Model's forces had been reinforced by two strong corps from Army Group H in Holland. Close to half a million Germans were braced to oppose our landings.

Over-all command in the West had now passed into the hands of Field Marshal General Albert Kesselring. Kesselring had been brought from Italy eleven days before to replace Field Marshal von Rundstedt, who had fallen from grace again when our seizure of the bridge at Remagen threw the entire German defense line into confusion. Kesselring's orders were as simple to understand as they were difficult to execute. Hitler told him to hold—to hold the line.

General Eisenhower had flown up from Supreme Headquarters at Reims on the day of the jump-off to go over last-minute preparations with Field Marshal Sir Bernard L. Montgomery. As commander of the 21st Army Group, the Field Marshal himself was in immediate control of Operation PLUNDER. Everything was in readiness. The troops had been briefed for their night assault across the Rhine. The plan called for artillery to open up exactly at eight o'clock and continue for an hour to saturate the enemy defenses. At 2100 hours, when the bombardment ceased, the First British commando Brigade would push off in assault boats, scramble up the opposite shore, and make for the key town of Wesel. Main crossings by two American and two British

infantry divisions would follow. Next morning, beginning at 1000 hours, an Allied airborne corps of two
divisions would be dropped at Wesel. Since standard
procedure is to use airborne troops in advance of an
amphibious assault, the Supreme Commander believed
this unexpected timing would add to the element of
surprise and hasten the disintegration of the defenders.

An air of great expectation hung over these proceedings. After nearly ten months of almost steady fighting
we had reached a decisive point in the war on the Western front. If the coming battle went as we hoped, we
should destroy in one swift campaign the greatest concentration of military forces remaining in Germany.
Toward evening, General Eisenhower went down to
the southern sector where the American Ninth Army
was in place for the jump-off. The Supreme Commander
had no orders to give. Those had all been issued. But he
had a special interest in watching the beginning of this
offensive. When our troops were still in England, he
had planned on a map that they would launch the final
campaign from this exact spot. The blueprint had come
to life.

In May, 1944, when the invasion of Normandy was a
month away, the Supreme Commander decided the
broad strategy by which Germany was to be defeated
in the West. His directive from the Combined Chiefs of
Staff, military High Command of Allied operations in
the global war, ordered him to invade the Continent and
strike to the heart of Germany. To the Staff at Supreme

Headquarters, Germany had two hearts. Berlin, as the capital of the Nazi citadel, was the political heart and the ultimate goal. But more vital to Germany's armies was the Ruhr, the industrial heart where cities and factories poured out steel and guns and fuel. Without the Ruhr, the army could not long exist. Since this area was vital to the German warmakers, we could be certain they would defend it with a great concentration of troops. To destroy the Ruhr would be to destroy a sizable part of the German army.

We were considering this at Supreme Headquarters in Bushy Park on the morning in early May after Field Marshal Montgomery had developed his scheme of maneuver for the operation in Normandy. The staff planners, locked in my office, presented to the Supreme Commander the various lines of action which might be adopted when we were strong enough on the Continent to break out of our lodgement area and begin the war of maneuver to defeat the German armies in the West.

The Supreme Commander agreed that the Ruhr was the key objective inside Germany. His broad plan was to drive into France along the line of the Seine and Loire rivers, destroying German strength as we liberated territory. Then, adopting as our main offensive line the route over the coastal plain of northern France, we would cross the Low Countries, slash into the fixed defenses of the Siegfried Line, and reach the Rhine north of the Ruhr. At the same time, if our campaign progressed as we hoped, we would push a secondary attack across the Rhine somewhere near the point where it is joined by the Moselle. If this supplementary drive worked out successfully, it would put our forces into the Frankfurt corridor. Over this favorable route, working in coordination with the attack from the north, we could stage a gigantic double envelopment of the Ruhr, destroying its defenders within an iron ring.

To most of the American officers at the staff conference that day, this promising plan had a personal appeal. We were remembering Count von Schlieffen, Chief of the German General Staff in the years before the First World War. He had written a book called *Cannae*, whose lessons we knew almost by heart. It was an analysis of Hannibal's great victory over the Romans, from which the scholarly soldier had developed his theory of the battle of annihilation by means of the double envelopment, encircling and destroying the enemy. The decisive German campaign at Tannenberg in August, 1914, was fought on this pattern, and the Schlieffen theories became subjects for exhaustive study in our own Army's General Service schools in the years after the war.

As products of these schools, the Supreme Commander, as well as many of his staff officers and commanders, were imbued with the idea of this type of wide, bold maneuver for decisive results. British officers on the Allied staff, veterans of earlier desert campaigns where maneuver was the keynote, had the same ideas. There was a nice sense of poetic justice in the prospect of applying the theories of an elder German strategist over Germany's sacred soil and on a scale which von Schlieffen could hardly have imagined.

General Eisenhower took a pencil to demonstrate the strategy by which we should approach and encircle the Ruhr. On the staff map he traced two main lines of advance. The first sprang from Normandy across northern France and Belgium, reaching the Rhine north of the Ruhr. From southern Normandy, a second line followed the Loire, dipped across the Seine below Paris, and then began converging toward the northern line of march to approach the Rhine just below the first. A third line broke off from the second in a southeasterly direction somewhere in eastern France. This was the offensive which we hoped might explode into Germany through the Frankfurt corridor. The line drove below the Ardennes and pushed for the Rhine in the general direction of Coblenz.

There, penciled on the map, was the draft of our grand strategy. In the months that followed, subsidiary plans were changed as the enemy revealed his own strategy—or lack of it—for countering our designs. But our broad advance across France and into Germany followed the original pattern. I doubt that there has ever been a campaign in history where actual operations fitted so closely the initial plan of a commander, adopted so far in advance. Long before we set foot in Europe and tested the enemy's strength in battle, we had decided on the blueprint for his defeat.

In the layman's mind, this one would scarcely be recognized as a "decision." It was rather a plan, an expression in concrete terms of the most effective and speedy way our operations should develop in the strategic sense.

Nevertheless, its effect was to give constant guidance to the great staffs and various commands charged with responsibility for working out every item of transport, of supply, of evacuation, of training, of replacement, and of organization that would finally make the dream come true.

It aimed at an unremitting offensive, concentrating power on the left until the Rhine was crossed, a rapid thrust across France to connect up with the invasion coming from the Mediterranean, a secondary crossing of the Rhine near Frankfurt to accomplish a double envelopment of the entire Ruhr, and, finally, a drive across Germany to meet the Russian advance. The conception colored and dictated our conclusions concerning the necessity and the proper objectives for the assault that was launched from the Mediterranean against the southern coast of France in August, 1944. This attack not only insured the speedy liberation of all southern France but, more important, it made possible, as was expected, a more rapid pouring of American strength into the main battle area—a result that advanced the end of the war by months.

The plan fixed, in a general way, the principal lines of communication—roads, railroads, and waterways—to which we gave priority in development and repair. It influenced the assignment of troops to the various Allied army groups and armies, and dictated the sequence of intermediate objectives all the way from Normandy to the Elbe. In sum, its effects were so profound upon everything we did that it must be considered one of the six major decisions which resulted in the speedy and amazing victory over the German armies in western Europe.

As March advanced toward the date of the big offensive, the Allied armies were at the peak of their power. The combat divisions were at full strength. The air force had grown to a weapon of decisive skill. General Eisenhower had some five million men at his disposal, charged with the aggressive spirit that only a sense of victory can bring. They were veterans now and they had the confidence of seasoned soldiers. They had met and beaten the best the Germans had to offer. They had shattered the legend of Nazi invincibility behind the Atlantic Wall and chased the enemy across France to the Siegfried Line. They had taken the desperate blow in the Ardennes and rebounded to drive the Germans through the Siegfried Line fortifications and across the Rhine. From February 8, when our offensive west of the river began, to the main crossing on March 23, we had captured 300,000 prisoners of war. We had robbed the Germans of twenty divisions, in addition to the numbers they had lost in killed and wounded.

The bridge we seized at Remagen on March 7 had unlocked the door to the Frankfurt corridor. Three American army corps were poised in the bridgehead ready to pace the northern attackers in the envelopment of the Ruhr. The swift capitulation of Cologne in early March had saved us five more divisions which could now be added to the weight of this offensive thrust. South of

Remagen, General Patton had ferried an entire infantry division across the Rhine in a surprise night assault on March 22. This bridgehead, too, was being rapidly consolidated to erupt into the Frankfurt area, seizing the bridges over the Main River.

In contrast to our own mounting power, the German forces had diminished steadily under the continuous mauling we had given them. Field Marshal Kesselring was faced with a difficult problem when he assumed command. With Allied troops holding a bridgehead south of the Ruhr and quite obviously preparing to seize another in the north, he had too few divisions to oppose both with any chance of success. The High Command's strategy was to hold the Ruhr. Expecting that the Americans in the Remagen bridgehead would strike north to attack the underbelly of this industrial area, he ordered Field Marshal von Model to move picked forces to hold us on the east-west line of the Sieg River. But Allied Supreme Headquarters had never intended its main breakout to go in that direction. Kesselring, although he expected a double envelopment of the Ruhr, mistook completely the intent of the south arm of the pincers. When General Bradley's forces erupted from their bridgehead on March 26, they raced south against weak resistance to pour into the Frankfurt corridor. Once on this easier terrain, they wheeled due north to strike toward Kassel, Paderborn, and the long arm of the Ninth Army swinging around the Ruhr to meet them.

After his capture, Field Marshal Kesselring told us some of his difficulties in carrying out Hitler's orders to hold a line across Germany. "In order to maintain a straighter line along the front," he said, "I would have used the troops in the Ruhr and given up the Ruhr to maintain the line." Then he added sharply, "But that was the crime of Remagen! It broke the front along the Rhine! Without that our divisions would have had a chance to refresh and get reinforcements so that they might have opposed you with a strength of eight thousand to nine thousand rather than an average strength of four thousand. We knew you regarded the Rhine as a great barrier and would pause to regroup. That would give *us* a chance to pause and regroup. The magnetic way in which the Remagen bridgehead drew these divisions prevented their being reinforced for the battle to stop the encirclement of the Ruhr."

There was more to Kesselring's problem than that. His troops were already beaten men. German soldiers who had managed to make their way back across the Rhine were exhausted and in no condition to stand the pounding of further air attack and ground assault. Yet he had no choice but to use them. Since February 8 there had never been a moment when the front was not on fire somewhere, needing more troops than even the most thorough combings of Germany could supply. New crises sucked up the ever-diminishing reserves. When the great Allied offensive began in the north, the troops on the ground had to fight on or surrender. There was no possibility of their being relieved.

Deterioration was spreading within the German army. The SS, the armored units, and the parachute Army, mostly fanatical Nazis, kept up their morale. But the Volksgrenadiers, poorly and too briefly trained, had little heart to continue the struggle. Their discouragement was mirrored in a captured document sent back from the front for the amusement of the Staff at Supreme Headquarters. It was a letter written late in January when von Rundstedt still commanded in the West by the Commanding General of the 47th Volksgrenadier Division to his corps headquarters. The harried commander complained, somewhat bitterly, we thought:

> Division wishes to report that the reward of a gift of a signed photograph of Field Marshal Rundstedt for individual combat has produced no result. No request for this award has been submitted.
>
> At the moment, this division does not expect a reward of this kind to stimulate shooting. Troops can only be encouraged to shoot by the creation of more equal conditions of combat.

Allied air power had been called upon to play a decisive role in preparing the way for the northern crossing of the Rhine. Although the Luftwaffe had gone into almost complete eclipse after its savage activity during the Ardennes counteroffensive, the appearance of its new jet planes in the battle area gave the Air Staff at Supreme Headquarters a major cause for concern. Germany was well ahead of the Allies in the development of these lightning-swift fighters, now modified from their original intent to carry a bomb or two. Because of their superior speed, it was difficult for our own planes to deal with them in the air. The danger was that the Germans would husband their still relatively small numbers for an all-out attack against our crossings.

The most practical defense worked out by our air force was to throw continuous attacks against the fields from which the jets took off. These planes required an extra-long runway, and the extended strips made their fields easy to spot. Beginning on March 21, our heavy bombers attacked every field within reach of the battle area. Many jet planes were destroyed on the ground, and the special runways were cratered into at least temporary uselessness. Pinpoint bombing of dumps storing their particular brand of fuel completed the measures that kept this powerful weapon from serious interference.

But the most spectacular air contribution was the great strategic bombing campaign which began on February 21. Our air planners had been convinced that it was possible to neutralize the Ruhr as a center of heavy industry by severing its transportation lines with the rest of Germany. The critical targets were eighteen railroad bridges and viaducts. Once these were knocked out, the air planners believed, the Ruhr would be almost completely isolated. During the next month, ten were destroyed and four more damaged. In addition to this perimeter bombing, transportation centers within the Ruhr itself were heavily attacked. Essen was saturated by 1,079 planes dropping 5,000 tons of bombs on March 11. Next day Dortmund received an even weightier blow of 5,487 tons from 1,108 planes. By

March 19, our reconnaissance reported that no traffic was moving anywhere within the Ruhr.

The weather, which had sharply curtailed our full use of air power through the autumn and winter, shifted to our side in March and April. Days were sunny and nights clear. In the last days before the main Rhine crossing, fighter-bombers of the tactical air forces flew the battle area, diving at supply dumps, strafing columns of troops and vehicles, pulverizing new defenses as quickly as the Germans could build them. Rocket-firing Typhoons combed over enemy barracks and stores. At the climax of these operations, in the four-day period beginning three days before the jump-off, the Allied Air Force flew 42,000 sorties from bases throughout Britain and the Continent. Two heavy raids were made on Berlin from Italy as part of the assault.

On the heels of this terrific dislocation from the air, and in the echo of the great artillery bombardment, the commandos pushed out in their assault boats at nine o'clock on the evening of March 23. As we hoped, the preliminary softening-up had dazed the defenders and kept them from massing coordinated resistance at the river. Assault waves of infantry, tanks, and guns poured on the opposite shore, and in their wake the Engineers pushed the first of the bridges across the Rhine. One unit performed the almost incredible feat of building a railroad bridge in eleven hours. The great anxiety of any amphibious landing—the speed of build-up on the opposite shore—filled Friday night and all the next day with tension as the two armies, American and British, ferried

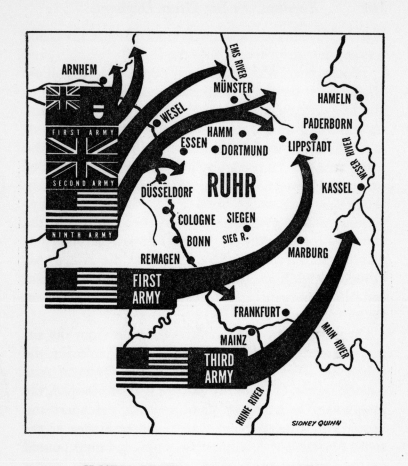

CLOSING PINCERS AROUND THE RUHR

the river in darkness. North of the British, the Canadian Army protected our position against any interference by the strong German forces in Holland.

Shortly before ten o'clock on Saturday morning, the big troop carriers began towing gliders over Wesel. Two divisions were flown in, the British 6th Airborne from East Anglia and the American 17th from fields near Paris. Although there were some losses due to anti-aircraft fire, the fighter cover swept all Luftwaffe opposition from the sky. Not a single transport or glider was bothered by hostile planes. The airborne divisions joined up with the ground forces, consolidation proceeded swiftly, and the bridgeheads were expanded. By Sunday, March 25, we were firmly established and reinforcements were pouring across by bridge and landing craft. On Wednesday, the entire force turned in strength toward the Ruhr.

American and British troops performed in perfect teamwork under Field Marshal Montgomery's command. For more than three months—since the enemy's counteroffensive through the Ardennes—the American Ninth Army had been part of his 21st Army Group. We were sometimes puzzled during the war to see comments in both American and British press that probed for some hidden significance in the assignment of American troops to a British commander. Such comments simply missed the point that General Eisenhower commanded an Allied force in which nationality was of no importance. Differences of equipment and supplies usually made it impractical to mix units smaller than a

corps, though in the airborne corps which landed at
Wesel an American and a British division worked
smoothly side by side. The assignment of the American
Ninth Army to the predominantly British Army group
commanded by Field Marshal Montgomery during the
Ruhr campaign was for the sole purpose of providing
sufficient weight of troops to insure success. After the
Ruhr was ringed, the Ninth Army reverted to General
Omar N. Bradley's 12th Army Group, where it was
more needed for forthcoming operations on that front
than by Field Marshal Montgomery in the north.

Although the Germans had correctly estimated our
principal intentions, they were unable to mount effective
counterattacks as our advance progressed. They knew
we meant to encircle the Ruhr. "But we did not expect
it so quickly," complained Col. Gen. Alfred Jodl, Chief
of Hitler's Armed Forces Staff, when we asked him for
comment after his capture at the end of hostilities. "We
hoped that von Model's forces could pin down your
armies for a time and prevent further advance at such
speed." We inquired how the Germans planned to stop
us. "We had no plan except to prevent a union of the
two Allied armies and stop the encirclement," Jodl admitted. "We were surprised by the rapid break-through
and had nothing to oppose it. From that time," he said
quite frankly, "we could no longer talk of a general
conduct of the war. We had no reserves and could exert
no control over the situation."

Kesselring tried. His efforts were mainly addressed to

urging Model to take decisive measures to stop the strong force which was by this time in the Frankfurt corridor on the lower wing of the double envelopment. "I differed with Field Marshal Model in the way he tried to stop this rapid advance south of the Ruhr," Kesselring said. "In my personal opinion, he should have started his attack further to the east, thereby cutting off the relatively weak points of your advance and restoring a north-south line, rather than allowing his flank to be turned as it was. By attacking too far west," Kesselring pointed out, "Model ran into a much thicker column and was unsuccessful. It is the point at which you strike that makes the difference. One battalion striking at the right point can do far more than a division at the wrong point."

Whatever the military soundness of Kesselring's comments, the advance up the Frankfurt corridor excited Jodl's admiration. "Strikingly daring and effectively executed," he said, "was the movement which took Frankfurt, Giessen, and Marburg to join the right wing of the northern army at Lippstadt. These were faultlessly executed operations, taken at a big risk."

Our troops entered Marburg on March 28, the day the northern force moved east in strength. Then the American First Army swung back west to meet the arc which the Ninth Army was curving down from the north. On April 1, the two armies made firm contact at Lippstadt. Within a rough circle some eighty miles in diameter, Field Marshal von Model was trapped with the bulk of the forces in Central Germany.

No moment of the war, unless it was the surrender, brought more elation to the Staff at Supreme Headquarters than the message which reported that the encirclement was complete. The closed ring had also brought full circle the strategy adopted in a time that seemed like ancient history now. We could not pause to enjoy the triumph. There was too much urgency required to plan the coming campaigns and to provide the masses of supply they would require. More bridges over the Rhine were rushed to speed traffic. Pipelines were laid under the river to carry gasoline to the spearheads that would soon be flushing Germans from the furthest corners of their homeland.

Kesselring ordered counterattacks to break the ring before it could be securely forged, and von Model's troops fought vigorously at first. They tried to cut their way out north through Hamm, in coordination with troops counterattacking from the outside. They dashed against the wall of Americans at Siegen in the south. But the ring was already too strong.

Then Hitler stepped in with orders. The Ruhr was to be treated as a fortress. Von Model would no longer try to break out but would defend the area against all attacks. According to Goering, after his capture, "the troops in the Ruhr were given instructions not to surrender under any circumstances. The Fuehrer was of the opinion," he added, "that Model could have defended the Ruhr better than he did."

But unless he counterattacked, there was very little Model could do against the strategy adopted by the

Supreme Commander. General Eisenhower had no intention of driving a heavy assault against the cities and factories. His instructions were to press in constantly, constricting the size of the ring until, in the end, a few of our divisions could starve the defenders into submission.

To take the Ruhr by storm would involve heavy casualties. There were no military fortifications in the area. None were needed. The great industrial section is entirely a built-up area in which towns and factories simply gave way to more towns and more factories. Had we tried to drive in a wedge, the German tactics would have been to resist from building to building, as Aachen had been defended. It was this vicious type of in-fighting that General Eisenhower was determined to avoid. The Germans could not get out, and we could now afford the troops to shrink the gradually diminishing ring. Our main advance halted only briefly to make sure the Ruhr was locked. Within a few days, Allied spearheads were a hundred miles to the east.

In Berlin, the High Command was desperately concerned with the danger to the Ruhr. But they hoped it could still serve an important military purpose. Jodl said their hope was to pin down as many Allied troops as possible, and Goering told us his Fuehrer thought the Ruhr might keep twenty of our divisions busy while Hitler busied himself with preparations for resistance elsewhere. Von Model, from his headquarters near Düsseldorf, sent a message to Berlin: He was still on the Rhine, and where was the High Command? German staff officers were flown into the area once or twice. One came out bearing a long report on military and economic conditions within the pocket which must have made discouraging reading. Although the Ruhr had been declared a fortress by Hitler, the area could not long support the tremendous military population suddenly added to its already crowded civilian cities and suburbs. Production in the factories ceased. Distribution inside the pocket broke down completely. The fact was that while the Ruhr was quite plentifully supplied when it was closed in, the Germans were unable to move fuel, ammunition, and food to the points where they were needed. There was plenty of ammunition but very often a particular locality had the wrong caliber handy and none that would fit the guns. Some of the tanks that were close to a good gasoline supply were immobilized by a lack of spare parts. Food was plentiful in some places. In others, the larder was bare. The curious anomaly developed that fuel dumps were destroyed to prevent their capture by Allied forces while not far away tanks and other vehicles were being blown up by the Germans because they had no fuel.

By April 13, disintegration set in among the trapped divisions. Resistance became more scattered, and the German troops began to give themselves up. Von Model radioed that he doubted he could hold out more than forty-eight hours, and the High Command sent him new orders. As Jodl recalled them, the troops within the pocket were to draw together into groups and hold out separately as long as possible. If this became impractical, then they were to try to break out or infiltrate their way through our positions. With unfailing optimism, the High Command even ordered these exhausted troops, once they had broken through, to attack the rear of our lines!

But then, on April 15, the defense simply fell apart. Converging attacks by our First and Ninth armies split the pocket at Hagen. Next day, the eastern half collapsed, and 80,000 prisoners were taken in twenty-four hours. Even radio communication with Berlin now was broken. The German High Command learned from our own broadcasts the outcome of Hitler's fortress strategy. The final capitulation came on April 18—just eighteen days after the ring was forged. Our bag was far greater than we had at first suspected. Early estimates put the pocketed troops at 200,000. Actually, 325,000 surrendered, with thirty generals among them. We destroyed twenty-one divisions, including three panzer, one panzergrenadier, and three parachute divisions. We could do no more than estimate the quantity of enemy matériel that fell into our hands.

We looked in vain for Field Marshal von Model among the prisoners. He was last seen by some of his men making his way across country on foot with a few staff officers. Months later, his Intelligence chief said the defeated commander had shot himself on April 21 in a wood near Duisburg, three days after the collapse of the pocket.

The all-out defense of the Ruhr had cost the enemy his last chance of reconstructing a coordinated defense of the German homeland. Except in Holland, which

Hitler had also declared a fortress, no strongly unified force remained. Had von Model's troops been ordered to withdraw and form another line, instead of inviting encirclement, it is possible they might have made our task far more difficult and costly in the weeks to come. The Ruhr had already lost its meaning as a production center. Perhaps, as Goering and Jodl said, Hitler believed the area could serve an important military purpose by pinning down our divisions. More probably, his strategy was the result of his deep distrust of some of his generals. If any order for retreat was given, he professed to believe they would act on it immediately instead of trying to hold on. As a result, when his withdrawal orders finally came, they were always too late. The troops were lost.

From his shifting headquarters, now in the East, now at Berchtesgaden, now in Berlin, Hitler still tried to keep tight rein on the moves of all his commanders, plotting maneuvers on his maps long after the areas they were to attack had been overrun by the Allies. All the futility of his frenetic leadership is displayed in a captured order which bore his signature. With their world crumbling about them, it must have been maddening to the German field commanders, already having the greatest difficult in maintaining contact with their own subordinate units, to read the following directive:

1. The Commanding Generals of Armies, Corps and Divisions will be personally responsible for *all* of the following type decisions or intentions reaching me early enough to enable me

to exercise influence on such decisions and for a possible coun-
terorder to reach the front-line troops in time:

a. Any decision involving an operational movement.

b. Any projected attack of division size or larger which is
not covered by general orders issued by Supreme Headquarters.

c. Any offensive action on an inactive front exceeding normal patrol activity and apt to draw the enemy's attention to
that sector.

d. Any projected movement of withdrawal or retreat.

e. Any contemplated abandonment of a position, a fortified
town or a fortress.

2. The Commanding Generals of Armies, Corps and Divisions, the Chiefs of Staff and every single General Staff officer
or staff officer will be personally responsible to me to see that
any report addressed to me directly or through channels will
contain nothing but the blunt truth. In the future I will dras-
tically punish any attempt at veiling facts, whether done on
purpose or through negligence.

(signed) Adolf Hitler.

There was now no longer question of the enemy's
rapid disintegration. In the first two weeks of April we
had taken 500,000 prisoners. By the end of the third
week, this number had doubled. As Intelligence summed
up the situation for the Staff at Supreme Headquarters,
"the paralysis which commenced in the body of Germany when the Remagen bridgehead was seized has
spread rapidly. It is now well up the spinal column. The
enemy in the West is no longer offering organized resistance except in the north and south of his so-called
line. And this is crumbling rapidly. An SS Panzer Army
has appeared without either Panzers or SS formations.
The whole thing is senseless. From every viewpoint it is

only a matter of time before organized resistance in Hitlerite Germany collapses completely. The German will go on fighting, with diminishing strength. We shall, perhaps, be faced with a campaign in the National Redoubt or in Norway. But nothing can now rectify the mistakes of Hitler and his staff officers or even partially relieve the situation. Enemy capabilities are, in fact, *nil*. But the greatest world war looks as though it will end, not by a total collapse (at any rate, not as long as Hitler and Himmler control affairs) but by a systematic annihilation of the German armed forces."

Still there was no consideration of surrender in the German High Command, though some of the generals must have thought of it wistfully. We asked General Jodl what discussions they had for surrender after the Ruhr pocket collapsed, and Jodl answered, "None. We did not discuss a general surrender." We asked then at what point surrender was first considered. "After Hitler's death," Jodl said.

So the Staff's estimate at Supreme Headquarters proved correct. After the Ruhr was taken, we were convinced there would be no surrender at all, so long as Hitler lived. Our feeling then was that we should be forced to destroy the remnants of the German army piece by piece, with the final possibility of a prolonged campaign in the rugged Alpine region of western Austria known as the National Redoubt. This we knew was the intent of mad Hitlerism. Even while the Ruhr fighting continued, photographs of the Redoubt area were building up evidence of new dugouts, extensive trenches, bunkers, and gun positions. Existing ditches and canals were being extended to form antitank obstacles.

The Supreme Commander was determined to end the war as quickly as possible. If it was the German intention to conduct a protracted, last-ditch defense, hopeless in itself but quite in keeping with the Hitler mentality, we must prevent it to save Allied lives. The Staff began to recast Allied plans and to point more forces toward an accelerated southern campaign to frustrate the Germans' schemes.

In some actions, the Germans still fought tenaciously. But mostly, they were very much as they had been in the last days of Tunisia, nearly two years before. Up near Tunis and Bizerte, when our attacks broke through and got behind them, they surrendered in droves. They were that way now in Germany.

I remember visiting a corps headquarters following the Ruhr collapse. It was an armored corps in the American Seventh Army zone, and I was surprised to find that the commander, Maj. Gen. Edward H. Brooks, had his own headquarters in advance of division headquarters. We were having lunch, and there was fighting going on in full view up the neighboring hill. Our artillery was firing overhead. I said, "You're getting pretty ambitious for a corps commander, aren't you?"

The General shrugged his shoulders and laughed. "Well, you've got to boot them along a little bit," he said, looking out the window to watch our shells bursting on positions from which the enemy was already withdrawing.

SITUATION REPORT

* * * * *

Now THE front was everywhere, and in that month of April Allied spearheads drove swift armored fingers against all enemy centers of resistance. On March 30, the Supreme Commander had broadcast a message to the German armies, pointing out the futility of further resistance, calling on them to surrender. There was no reply. In the far north of Europe, as the month rolled on, British troops of the Second Army pushed their way into Denmark and lifted the occupation that nation had suffered since 1940. In the south, troops of the American Seventh Army pushed to the Brenner Pass and there met the American Fifth Army coming north to make a link-up of European and Mediterranean forces. The April spring was soft and mild, with clear skies for the planes to work in. Far behind the lines Paris was in bloom. The last flying bomb fell on London in mid-April, landing near the Marble Arch. The civilian population of Holland was desperate for want of food, but the German commander there, although he agreed to allow us to drop supplies of food and medicine, refused to consider the surrender of his hopeless army. Russian forces crossed the Oder River on April 17 and raced the thirty miles to Berlin to beat down the bitter, house-to-house resistance of the German garrison. On April 12, General Eisenhower visited General Bradley and together they motored to General Patton's Third Army field headquarters. They visited the first horror camp the Supreme Commander had seen, Ohrdruf near the town of Gotha. "I have never been able to describe my emotional reactions when I first came face to face with indisputable evidence of Nazi brutality and ruthless disregard of every shred of decency," he wrote later. That evening from Patton's headquarters he sent a message to General Marshall, asking that delegations both of members of Congress and newspaper editors be flow to Germany to see these spots of degradation with their own eyes. He wanted to make sure that never in the future would it be said the reports of such unbelievable brutality could be labeled as propaganda. That same afternoon the Supreme Commander had seen an unforgettable sight of a different character—the Nazi treasure trove in the village of Merkers. There, in a salt mine half a mile deep, troops of the Third Army had found gold in coins, bars, and beaten down ornaments valued at some $250,000,000, and paintings which represented many of the art treasures of Europe. General Eisenhower and General Bradley spent that night at General Patton's headquarters. Some time after they had gone to bed, General Patton awakened them. He had just heard over the radio that

President Roosevelt was dead. Whispers of surrender attempts were coming now as April approached its close. Himmler attempted to reach Prime Minister Churchill through Count Bernadotte of Sweden. The Germans hoped to surrender to the West. In Berlin, the situation had reached its last hours of desperation. Hitler was telling his associates that he would never be taken. On the afternoon of Monday, April 30, he shot himself in the deep bunker near the Reichschancellery. A few days later resistance ceased in the Nazi capital. Now the advances were overrunning prisoner-of-war camps deep in Germany where Allied troops were held. Transport planes and converted bombers returning from supply missions to the combat fronts flew these men back and they were placed immediately in rest camps in the north of France and in Belgium where they were given medical care and the food which had been criminally lacking in the prisoner-of-war camps the last few weeks. At Lucky Strike, the American camp near Le Havre, at one time there were 47,000 American soldiers undergoing rehabilitation before the voyage home. Now the surrenders were to begin in earnest. Late in April, on the 29th, the first of these came: All German forces in Italy capitulated to the Allied commander on the only terms acceptable to the Supreme Commander—unconditional surrender. It was a question of days until the last soldier in the German Reich would lay down his arms.

6. The Only Way
It Could End

FROM the day our invasion broke over the beaches of Normandy, the goal of every Allied soldier had been Berlin. The Supreme Commander, the Staff, and all the troops shared a driving ambition to seal the defeat of Nazi Germany by seizing the capital of the Reich itself. During our planning days in England, there seemed every reason to believe that after the Ruhr was encircled and its troops destroyed, we could end the war by taking Germany's political heart—Berlin.

By the end of January, 1945, the German Government was evacuating the capital, fleeing to temporary safety in the Thuringian Forest and south to Hitler's own retreat in mountainous Berchtesgaden. Deserted by its Nazi masters and ruined by our massive air bombardments, the city was becoming a shell—an empty symbol of the Nazis' brutal grandeur. It was losing all meaning as a military objective.

Our task was to end the war swiftly and conclusively.

Berlin was no longer a major factor in reaching that end. Every plan, decision, and purpose of the Allied command was determined always by one inflexible rule— "Destroy the German forces, speedily and completely." By April 1, when the ring snapped shut around the Ruhr, we were convinced that there would be no general surrender so long as Hitler remained in command. The war would be finished now by only one means: We must root out and destroy every remnant of military strength until no organized force remained in Germany to carry on the fight.

Faced with this practical reality as March drew to a close, the Supreme Commander approved plans designed for final decisive results. Berlin was abandoned as an objective. Our power would first be put behind an immediate concentrated drive of General Bradley's First, Third, and Ninth armies thrusting eastward across the central German plain in the direction of Leipzig and Dresden. Somewhere out there we would meet the oncoming Russians. Once our fronts joined, a solid line from west to east would divide Germany's military forces. We could then complete their destruction in detail.

Alongside this principal drive, Field Marshal Montgomery's armies would push north to Holland, to Bremen and Hamburg, to the Baltic. With the capture of these ports, the last vestiges of the U-boat menace would be destroyed, and Germany's forces in Denmark and Norway severed from the Reich. Somewhere in that zone, too, we should join the Russians.

In the south, General Devers' forces, and perhaps the Third Army, would drive through Nürnberg and Regensburg, following the Danube Valley into Austria. There we should meet the southern wing of the Red Army coming in from the Balkans. Besides destroying considerable German forces east of Munich, this drive would also cut off the Alpine area containing the mysterious National Redoubt, where we had every reason to believe the Nazis intended to make their last stand among the crags. Around Berchtesgaden and Salzburg, we should run down the principal government departments fled from Berlin. Beating through the tortuous terrain of the Austrian Alps, our forces would destroy the safety of this promised Nazi refuge.

On April 4, with Fortress Ruhr walled around by our troops, the great Allied drive roared eastward through Kassel. In the thirty-three days that followed, our forces penetrated to every corner of the Reich, while German soldiers, sometimes after bitter fighting, more often in sullen relief, threw down their arms. Those thirty-three days of searching activity saw Allied might at the peak of its power in Europe. At times there were as many as ten simultaneous full-scale armored drives rolling up German troops from the Baltic to the Brenner Pass, while our planes rode ahead and on the flanks to seek out and attack enemy resistance. These slashing, relentless offensives gave the enemy no opportunity to rally his forces anywhere for a final stand. When Col. Gen. Alfred Jodl, Chief of Hitler's Armed Forces Staff, surrendered at Supreme Headquarters in the early hours of

May 7, he was delivering up the remains of an army which had been beaten more thoroughly and more disastrously than any major force in history.

Instead of wasting time and lives on ruined Berlin, the Allies had put an end to all German resistance in thirty-three climactic days by the only means the Nazis would accept. This sixth and last great decision by the Supreme Commander insured the destruction of Hitler's armies in the West.

In all our projected operations, we visualized an eventual meeting with the Russians driving west. While the fronts were far apart, the offensives of the Western Allies and the Red Army could be pursued independently. In both spheres, German armies were being destroyed, grinding up Nazi reserves. But toward the close of December, with the Ardennes counteroffensive under control and the campaigns for crossing the Rhine in prospect, General Eisenhower believed the time had come when definite mutual understanding was required. A meeting in Moscow was arranged by President Roosevelt, and the Supreme Commander sent his deputy, Air Chief Marshal Sir Arthur W. Tedder, at the head of a military mission to confer with Marshal Stalin.

Our plans to close with the Germans both west and east of the Rhine were fully disclosed to the Soviet High Command. Marshal Stalin revealed his own scheme of operations—a gigantic spring offensive in which 150 to 160 Red Army divisions would be turned against the Germans with the intent of driving them entirely from their eastern conquests. Marshal Stalin volunteered that if weather delayed the big offensive, he would order local actions of sufficient size to prevent the Germans from transferring major forces to the Western front.

As soon as the Supreme Commander's strategy for the final knock-out blow in Germany was decided, Marshal Stalin was told of our plans, which fitted with his own. Immediate steps were then taken to agree on a system of signals for mutual recognition between the two armies when they should meet. Moreover, we hoped to effect the junction along an easily recognizable terrain feature, in order to facilitate cooperation and recognition by troops of both armies. The River Elbe was fortunately located for this purpose. Since it was quite impossible to predict the exact circumstances under which the meeting would take place, it was of the utmost importance that recognition signals were well understood by both armies to guard against the tragedy that mistaken identity might mar this long-anticipated junction by a clash of arms. It was not till April 20, five days before the first actual contact at Torgau, that agreement was finally reached.

It has been suggested on a great many occasions and from many sources that we deliberately avoided Berlin because of a political agreement that the Russians, rather than the Western Allies, were to capture the Nazi capital. Nothing could be further from the truth. There was no political consideration involved and there was no agreement on this score with the Russians. General Eisenhower's decision to destroy the remaining enemy forces throughout Germany and, above all, to seal off the National Redoubt, was based on a realistic estimate of the military situation. The fact that the Red Army was only some thirty miles from the city made a thrust by our armies toward the capital even more futile as part of the over-all military strategy to end the war. The only importance Berlin now possessed was the destruction of German forces rallying for its defense. The Red Army could be counted on to take care of that job.

Battles are fought to defeat armies, to destroy the enemy's ability to go on fighting. Only when a port, such as Cherbourg, or an area, such as the Ruhr, is so vital to the enemy that it is protected with large numbers of troops, or when a particular locality, such as Foggia in Italy, provides great advantages for the further development of a campaign, are "terrain objectives" of justified military importance. With the German Government evacuated, Berlin was a terrain objective empty of meaning. To send our armies crashing into its western suburbs could have no tactical significance. General Eisenhower felt that such a campaign would have its only importance in headlines, and no battle was ever fought by the Allied Expeditionary Force for headlines.

The great double envelopment of the Ruhr had left jagged holes in the German defenses in the north and center of Germany. Twenty-one divisions, desperately needed by the Western Commander in Chief, Field Marshal General Albert Kesselring, were securely locked in the pocket. As we pushed into the interior of Germany during the first week in April, there was nothing Kesselring could do to form a coordinated defense against our advance. His communications were breaking down. Information about the positions of his own troops filtered into his command post hours and days late. By the time he could issue orders on the basis of his battle map, the situation had already been scrambled by advancing Allied spearheads.

General Jodl told us that from the time the Ruhr was encircled, the High Command could no longer control the situation. The reserves were used up. Our own maps at Supreme Headquarters revealed the enemy situation in detail, Holland, with a major German force of some thirteen good divisions, had been declared a fortress by Hitler. This meant that no call could be made on its garrison to fight the battle of Germany. A few divisions clustered around Bremen and the approaches of the Baltic. Some were gathering in the Harz Mountains, where General Wenk had been ordered to improvise a new Eleventh Army in the shelter of hilly, forested terrain. South of Chemnitz and Jena, a few divisions held some semblance of a line. On the other hand, it was true that ten new divisions had appeared in the West, three of them old friends reborn after destruction and seven which were fresh identifications. They were a very mixed lot but they did represent considerable fighting strength.

In these last days, the Germans were hastily compressing remnants of old divisions broken in battle, into new units, often under names calculated to inspire flagging spirits by an appeal to brighter moments in the history of the Reich. Bold names, like Jutland, Franken, Scharnhorst, Von Huetten, Potsdam, von Clausewitz, were dragged from the books. Legend and Richard Wagner together must have contributed Niebelungen, a new SS infantry unit. With its ships almost gone, the Navy provided a source of manpower, and numbered divisions called Naval Infantry appeared. A division or two was scraped together from V-weapon crews, now that their launching sites were gone.

The mass of this manpower, ill-trained and ill-assorted as much of it was, held the possibility of prolonged resistance, particularly if it could gain the crags and canyons of southern Germany, the site of the National Redoubt. As the Staff at Supreme Headquarters estimated the final German score, when the country was cut in half by the junctions with the Russians, there would be approximately fifty divisions in the north, counting those isolated in Norway, Latvian Courland (where Hitler inexplicably abandoned eighteen to destruction by the Russians), and East Prussia. Below the dividing line, with the forces remaining on the Italian front, about one hundred divisions would remain. In this area, however, the bulk of German armor and SS formations was concentrated. Whether they had been drawn there as part of a strategic plan or simply by chance, the presence of these strongest forces in the Hitler arsenal gave added importance to seizing the National Redoubt before its defenses could be fully developed.

The whole plan of the National Redoubt remained something of an unknown quantity to the Staff in the early spring of 1945. In fact, the full extent of Hitler's plans for this region has never been fully revealed. The defense of a mountain stronghold follows no regular, well-defined pattern. Reconnaissance photographs showed that the Germans were installing extensive bunkers in the neighborhood of Berchtesgaden, though these were by no means finished. There was also an increase in antiaircraft protection. Feverish activity was now reported along the Danube River around Singen, Ulm, Regensburg, and Passau. Munich, shrine of the Nazi party, was being converted into one of Hitler's fortresses. We were told the city would be fought for street by street, and preparations there were said to exceed any defenses set up in Berlin.

The mystery of the National Redoubt deepened when several German general officer prisoners swore they had never heard of any organized large-scale defense positions in the Alps. All were German Army—Wehrmacht—rather than SS generals, and we were inclined to believe them, particularly when they agreed bitterly that a final withdrawal there was certainly consistent with National Socialist strategy and in all probability a part of it. Their guess was that the Wehrmacht would be directed to sacrifice itself by delaying actions outside the area, while SS formations holed up as the garrison. They thought the communications and supply situation in the Alpine region had been well enough organized in recent months so that this natural stronghold could be maintained as an independent fortress for any period up to a year.

By mid-April we knew definitely that all but the advance operational elements of the High Command and the military ministries had moved to Berchtesgaden, taking their records and equipment with them. The bunkers we heard of, and saw, in photographs were elaborate concrete command posts to house their administrative set-up. One plan that fell into our hands called for a heavily reinforced concrete bunker with three stories above ground and four below. The Fuehrer liked lots of concrete between himself and our bombers. Under the circumstances, this state of mind can hardly be considered unreasonable.

By mid-April, our thrust into the Thuringian Forest had sent the fugitive government departments sheltered there in full flight to join the rest of the ministries at Berchtesgaden. For some of them, the move was made just too late. Our troops overran their headquarters, seizing staffs and records intact. By now, Berchtesgaden was the center of the German civilian and military government. Even the diplomatic corps had moved in that direction.

By the end of the first week in April, the offensives of the three American armies were far to the East. The Ninth Army, on the northern flank, reached the Elbe River south of Magdeburg on April 11. That day the First Army was well into its offensive south of the Harz Mountains, where General Wenk was trying to whip his German Eleventh Army into some sort of shape, and one of General Patton's Third Army spearheads further south was surrounding Weimar, birthplace of the ill-fated republic formed at the close of the First World War. No opposition more serious than road-blocks was encountered by General Patton's troops up to this point. Erfurt and Jena were cleared on April 12 and 13, and our armor entered the outskirts of Chemnitz, where resistance stiffened. The enemy held this town as a pivot while the Germans swung back into the mountains along the Czechoslovakian frontier.

Back in the Ninth Army sector, three bridgeheads were pushed over the Elbe near Magdeburg, Wittenbirge, and Barby, but on April 15, in one of those unpredictable resurgences of fierce German opposition, the first two were driven in. The third, at Barby, held firm. Germans fought hard for Magdeburg. It was April 19 when the city fell.

The First Army was working its way around the Harz Mountains in the type of encircling maneuver which was so attractive to American commanders throughout the war. Dessau, just south of the confluence of the Elbe and Mulde rivers, was taken on April 14, and the encirclement was nearly completed. The ten thousand German troops pocketed in the difficult terrain tried desperately to keep open an eastern escape route toward Bernburg. The ring was finally closed on April 18. Even a wildly spectacular fifty-mile dash through Allied-held territory by the von Clausewitz Panzer Division failed to rescue the trapped Eleventh Army, and most of the von Clausewitz was added to the bag. General Wenk managed to escape, turning up in the last days at the head of the Twelfth Panzer Army.

Hitler had put great store by the promise of General Wenk's Eleventh Army, so Jodl told us later on. It was about all he had in the center. There were bits of the Replacement Army in the Kassel area—"shadow divisions," Jodl called them—with few vehicles or artillery but strong in infantry. These and some panzer replacement divisions were cannibalized to fill the dwindling ranks of the fighting formations. "Otherwise, we had no fresh troops in the strict sense," Jodl said. "We had a few engineer and cyclist units. Improvised forces, all these, to use in localized operations under the defense commands. Wenk's was the only real force."

At first, they planned to have Wenk counterattack westward in the hope of relieving Field Marshal von Model in the Ruhr pocket. When the impracticality of this measure became obvious, Wenk was directed to attack at the northern edge of the Thuringian Forest, around Eisenach. Before this could be started, Wenk was in a pocket himself. "I never believed we could assemble Wenk's army in time," Jodl said frankly. "It would not be ready while we still held the Harz. That is what in fact happened."

The American First Army pushed on to take Leipzig on April 19. The outflanked Germans voluntarily withdrew the salient they had kept between Leipzig and Halle, and we moved up to the Mulde. Further south— the Third Army had crossed into Czechoslovakia on April 18. The center front was restless with activity.

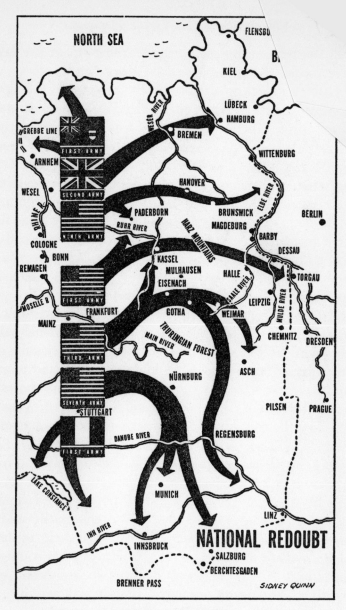

THE FINAL TRIUMPH OF WESTERN ALLIED ARMS

193

While General Bradley's armies were clearing out resistance and moving to their meeting with the Russians, the northern group under Field Marshal Montgomery had pushed northwest in early April. Two sweeping arms were directed at Bremen and Hamburg. A third, formed by the Canadian Army, pushed through Arnhem to test the walls of Hitler's Fortress Holland. Field Marshal Montgomery's forces reached the Elbe at Lauenburg on April 19 and Harburg on the south bank opposite Hamburg next day. On April 22, the southern prong was at Bremen.

The Canadians met heavy going at first with veteran units of the First Parachute Army in North Holland. Then resistance softened, and our forces reached the sea on April 15. Operations further west went equally well till the enemy withdrew behind the Grebbe Line and threatened to widen the flooded area by opening the dikes again. Field Marshal Montgomery believed, and the Supreme Commander agreed, that to force the barrier would only bring added misery to the Dutch population without accomplishing any important tactical purpose. The Germans were effectively cut off from contributing their services within Germany.

While operations continued in the north, the 6th Army Group with the American Seventh and French First armies in the southern sector of the front advanced rapidly eastward to Schweinfurt, Karlsruhe, Baden-Baden, and Stuttgart. Nürnberg fell on April 21, and the Seventh Army pushed south toward Munich. The Third Army, meanwhile, was roaring down the Danube Val-

ley and by April 25 had its first bridgehead over the
river near Regensburg.

But the spotlight of April 25 shone on the American
First Army beyond Leipzig. That Wednesday after-
noon, a patrol of the 273d Regiment, 69th Infantry
Division, moved out from the Mulde. Pushing east, these
American troops made the first contact with the Red
Army at Torgau on the River Elbe when they met for-
ward elements of the Russian 58th Guards Division. The
time was 4:40 P.M.

This long-waited event which at last cut the German
armies in two was almost too much for the analytically
minded officers of our Intelligence division. In the following estimate describing the enemy's dwindling future, they rose to lyrical heights quite unusual for G-2:

The historic moment has arrived. The attacking forces of the
Western and Eastern Armies of the Allies have met in the
heart of the Reich. Germany is divided in two, and our advance
toward Linz bids fair to dismember the rabble that remains of
the Wehrmacht still further. We shall then have three major
pockets. And a fourth, the blazing ruins of the Reich capital,
with Hitler probably in the rubble, too. If this is so, then he
can have no effective control of the battles of the pockets other
than his own. Furthermore, he has at last reached the level of
command which is more suited to him—streetfighting with
Volkssturm platoons. No longer shall we see that brilliant
strategy of the master brain leaving armies isolated all over
Europe, from Courland to Italy and from Norway to Jugo-
slavia. As each day passes, the state of the enemy deteriorates
and his stomach for fighting grows less. Surrenders increase,
led in some instances by generals. The enemy supply situation
is catastrophic, and he is living on what little fat remains to

him. Production of war material is totally inadequate to meet a small percentage of the requirements of the enemy.

But what happens next? From all accounts the "government" is settling in snugly among the Edelweiss of the Austrian Alps. From here it will presumably carry on the farce of keeping what remains of the wobbling Axis alive, while it pushes over the border of Switzerland its worn-out tools such as Pétain. The policy is plain: To sow hopefully last-minute discord among the Allies. Hitler to be martyred, perhaps, in Berlin as the man who fought the Bolshevik menace to the last. Himmler, apparently, trying to surrender to the West in order to play the Americans and British off against the Russians. Goering has a heart attack, as well he might. Goebbels presumably stumps in a bunker with Hitler. Ribbentrop is finished. It is fatuous. But it is tragic, too, that five men could create such misery and destruction to humanity and that no punishment could ever suffice to answer for their crimes.

Air Intelligence had a wry comment to add: "If Goering has left, as reported, the German Air Force should have less difficulty squeezing itself into the shrinking area in which it can operate. The removal of even such a large body, however, does not begin to solve the accommodations problem."

It is only fair to say that Intelligence had spoken of the Reichsmarshal and other German personalities mentioned with much more respect in their summaries a few months before.

On April 30, I had a personal talk with another of the iniquitous crew, Arthur Seyss-Inquart, the Nazi commissioner for Holland. The state of western Holland's population had grown desperate. Privations already imposed by the Nazis had been increased by the isolation of this unliberated section, and we were determined to get food and supplies to the people. We had no doubt that military operations on our part would induce the Nazis to open more dikes and increase the flooded area, destroying its fertility for years. General Blaskowitz, the military commander, was warned that such action would put a dark stain on his record, and we pointed out that nothing he could do in holding Holland would have the slightest influence in delaying the inevitable collapse of Germany.

It was Seyss-Inquart himself who proposed a compromise. If the Allied forces would promise to advance no further into Holland, the Germans would cooperate in getting relief supplies to the people. General Eisenhower directed me to go to the headquarters of the Canadian Army on the Grebbe Line to complete arrangements for this operation of mercy.

Seyss-Inquart came into our lines, accompanied by German Army, Navy, and Air officers. We told him what we wanted—to send in food and supplies by air drops, sea and land deliveries. He agreed in part and objected to some of the proposals. His requirements were more rigid than I thought necessary, but getting in the food was what counted. We made our bargain, and the food drops began immediately.

But there was another purpose in the back of our minds. General Eisenhower hoped this meeting might be used to induce the enemy to surrender the force in Holland, and I had a private talk with Seyss-Inquart and one or two of his advisers. The Nazi leader listened to the proposal and shook his head. He understood the situation and, while he did not say so, I knew he realized there was no hope for Germany. But he said surrender was a question for the military commander, Blaskowitz. He had no authority. Blaskowitz refused to surrender while resistance continued inside Germany.

Seyss-Inquart appeared inflexible. But a few minutes later his senior deputy, a German doctor, asked to talk with us alone. He was a Saxon and he begged us to resume the conversation with Seyss-Inquart. It was nothing to him personally, the doctor said. He had lost his wife and sons and he cared nothing for his own future. But he felt that many lives might be saved by resuming the conversation. We were more than willing.

Seyss-Inquart returned to the room and sat down. He was quite impervious to any appeal to reason. It was a matter for the military commander, Blaskowitz, or for Hitler, he repeated. Then we dropped all reserve.

"I wonder if you realize that I am giving you your last chance," I said.

He looked at me sharply and nodded. "Yes, I realize that."

I said, "The consequences to you yourself will be serious. You know what your acts have been here. You know the feeling of the Dutch people toward you. You know you will probably be shot."

He hesitated for only a moment and then said with a certain grim bravado, "That leaves me cold."

The obvious answer was, "It usually does." On this note the conversation ended.

The thirty-three days were running out now. Probing fingers of our armored divisions thrust deep into each soft spot in the German defenses. During the week that ended May 6, developments occurred so rapidly that they can hardly be catalogued in chronological order. This period was a single unit of time for the Supreme Commander and the Staff. Scarcely anyone left headquarters. We ate when we felt hungry, slept when we could no longer keep awake. Twelve o'clock on the dial of a watch might mean noon or midnight. A man looked toward the window to find out.

Hamburg fell to Field Marshal Montgomery's forces on May 3. Other British forces had dashed across Schleswig-Holstein to the Baltic and entered Lübeck on May 2, sealing off the enemy garrison in Denmark. Now the Red Army advance was throwing routed Germans back against our lines all along the front. One American corps took 300,000 German prisoners of war in a single period of twenty-four hours. On May 4, Field Marshal Montgomery accepted the surrender of all German forces in northwest Germany, including the neighboring islands, Denmark, Schleswig-Holstein, and Fortress Holland. By five miserable days, Seyss-Inquart had lost his last chance to show the slightest magnanimity of heart or concern for useless human suffering.

Our drive against the German forces remaining in the southeast had gained momentum like an avalanche. On the last day of April, Munich fell after brisk fighting but without the street-by-street defense we had been warned to expect. Our line now ran roughly along the

Lech River, north to Donauwörth, then followed the Danube to the Austrian frontier. But the German armies were already in an advanced state of collapse, streaming away toward the mountains. By the first day of May, we had reached the Isar River along its whole length from Munich to its confluence with the Danube.

Now our forces stormed into the National Redoubt, infantry leading armor through this difficult terrain. Whatever the Nazi plans had been for fanatical, last-ditch resistance in this area, they were frustrated by our swift advance. Innsbruck was cleared May 3. Next day Salzburg fell, and then our forces overran Berchtesgaden, the last stronghold of the Nazi Government. By May 5, it was all over in the south. The remaining troops surrendered unconditionally.

But there was a Götterdämmerung, after all, among the crags, though a rather sorry one. The northern slopes of the Alps yielded a rich harvest of German general officers. Many names from the days when Nazi blitzkrieg was running free over helpless peoples now were entered on the books of our prisoner of war cages. Six field marshals headed the list—von Leeb, von Weichs, List, Milch, Sperrle, and von Kleist—followed by numbers of smaller fry. Finally, there was Field Marshal von Rundstedt himself, his face still frozen and impassive, his monocle still firm in a Prussian eye.

Only a few square miles of Germany remained which had not been wiped clean of resistance—an alp or two, an island here and there. Hitler was dead, a suicide in Berlin three days before the city fell to the Russians on

May 2. General Jodl told us his version of the last tortured days of April, with Hitler peering at his maps and
radioing impossible orders to formless armies.

Jodl saw Hitler last, he said, in the bunker before the
Reichschancellery where the Nazi leader died. It was
Monday, April 23, when he left, carrying the Fuehrer's
latest orders to execute. We asked him curiously what
the man could have been planning while his world fell
in flames. "Wenk's Twelfth Army was to turn around,
defend on the Elbe and attack in the direction of Potsdam," Jodl said. Wenk was still engaged with the Russians. "The Ninth Army was encircled north of Kottbus.
It was to break out and join the Twelfth Army. At the
same time, with parts of another army group north of
Berlin, we were to attack south by way of Oranienburg
in the direction of Spandau."

Such moves were impossible, of course. Jodl saw
Goebbels outside the conference room after taking leave
of his Fuehrer. They talked of attempting to block the
encirclement of Berlin which was almost complete, or
of trying to tear open the ring once it was formed. "We
could not stop the Americans on the Elbe," Jodl said,
"but Keitel and I were to strike east to try and fight a
last battle around Berlin. Keitel was to command the
campaign."

There was really nothing Jodl could do after he left
Berlin. He had no communications, no means of rallying forces. By circuitous and furtive night marches he
made his way to the Baltic and finally to Flensburg in
Schleswig-Holstein, dodging first the Russians and then

the British when he got into the zone of the Twenty-first Army Group. He was in communication with Hitler by high-frequency radio till the end.

The last message from the embattled Fuehrer reached Jodl during the night of April 29/30. Hitler needed information to plot further phantom operations. "How is the attack going at Oranienburg?" . . . "Where is Wenk's advance column?" . . . "What is the situation of the Ninth Army?" These were some of the questions Hitler asked. Jodl hardly knew the answers himself but that night he radioed his own estimate of the general military situation. He could hold out little hope.

They got the news of Hitler's death in a radio from Martin Bormann—still in Berlin—addressed to Grand Admiral Doenitz on May 1. "Fuehrer gestern 1530 verschieden," Jodl said the message read. "Fuehrer died 3:30 P.M. yesterday." There was a second message, Jodl remembered, which announced that Hitler had passed his ragged mantle of German leadership to Doenitz. Jodl gave us the text of this message to Admiral Doenitz from memory: "Hitler provided for you to be President, Goebbels Chancellor, Seyss-Inquart Foreign Minister, Bormann Interior Minister. Leave it to you to tell the people. Will try to get to you." Bormann and Goebbels signed that one togther, Jodl said. It was the last word from Berlin.

The surrender conferences at Supreme Headquarters in Reims began on the evening of May 5 with the arrival of Admiral Hans von Friedeburg, bearing an olive branch from the man Hitler had designated as president of the German Reich, Grand Admiral Doenitz. The details of the surrender are well known—the attempt to stall, the efforts to surrender to the Western Allies while continuing hostilities with Russia. All these maneuvers met with the blunt reply that the only terms we would consider were unconditional surrender to all the Allies.

But there is one incident which has never been told. It gives final confirmation to the soundness of the Supreme Commander's decision to break up the German armies in the field so thoroughly that, when the time came to talk surrender, the Nazis would have no bargaining force left in arms.

While no military units worthy of the name remained within Germany itself, there were sizable German military and civilian groups in Czechoslovakia and the Balkans. Von Friedeburg's plane from Flensburg was grounded by weather at Brussels that morning of May 5. As he was completing the journey to Reims by car, a telephone message was received from Field Marshal Montgomery's headquarters, saying that von Friedeburg would attempt to delay actual surrender in order to rescue these forces from capture by the Russians.

Since every additional day we fought meant casualties to our own troops, the Supreme Commander was determined to obtain general surrender without delay. The Germans were in no position to resist, and he had no intention of prolonging hostilities by negotiation. We hastily prepared a map showing accurately our own and the German positions. But we added two entirely imaginary planned attacks, indicated by large red arrows. One sprang from our own front, the other from the Russian, converging to cut off the remaining German forces.

The map was lying on my desk when General Strong, Chief of Intelligence at Supreme Headquarters, brought von Friedeburg to my office. Only the three of us were present. Friedeburg and I did most of the talking, with General Strong as interpreter. As Field Marshal Montgomery had predicted, Friedeburg's game was to play for time. When we repeated the terms to him, he insisted that he had no authority to sign a general surrender. His eyes went several times to the map on my desk. Finally I handed it to him. "Obviously," I said, "you do not entirely realize the hopelessness of the German position."

He looked for a full minute at the large red attack arrows that apparently spelled the end of the last German armies in the field. Then tears came to his eyes, and he asked permission to send a message to Admiral Doenitz. He had no code with him, so the message was sent in Allied code to Field Marshal Montgomery's headquarters. From there it was flown to Flensburg. What von Friedeburg reported had immediate effect. Doenitz sent word that General Jodl was coming to Reims.

Jodl arrived at Supreme Headquarters at 5:30 on the afternoon of May 6. We let him talk things over alone with von Friedeburg for a time, and then I received them in my office with General Strong again acting as interpreter. Jodl was quite willing to surrender to the Western Allies, but not to the Russians. Then he asked for forty-eight hours to consider things and to get German soldiers and civilians out of the path of the Red Army in the south.

On General Eisenhower's instructions he was informed flatly that only unconditional surrender to both Eastern and Western Allies was acceptable. The Supreme Commander's ultimatum was: Unless these terms are accepted by midnight, in forty-eight hours the Allied front will be sealed. No more Germans of any description will be permitted to surrender to the Western Allies. This convinced Jodl of the futility of temporizing longer. His message went off to Admiral Doenitz.

Not long after midnight, Doenitz' reply was received, authorizing Jodl to sign for Germany. The final ceremony took place in the war room at Supreme Headquarters, lined with the battle maps that charted Germany's defeat. At 0241 hours on the morning of Monday, May 7, 1945, Jodl put his name to the document which acknowledged the official end of Hitler's reign of terror. The Supreme Commander could now report to the Combined Chiefs of Staff that his mission had been accomplished—one day more than eleven months after the Allied Expeditionary Force hit the beaches of Normandy.

To the personnel at Supreme Headquarters, responsible for the broad plans on which our victory was won, the final surrender was a time not of elation but of deepest satisfaction. Never once since our Headquarters came into being in London on February 12, 1944, had our unity of purpose been broken. We were a team of

American and British officers, with nationality forgotten to an extent which could never be realized by any man who was not part of our daily striving.

The Anglo-American Staff functioned as a complete, integral unit under the Supreme Commander. At times we disagreed—naturally. But we disagreed frankly as individuals, not as Britons and Americans. We were able to argue, to the last point of resistance, an honest difference of opinion without slackening in the least our united effort against the common enemy.

Out of this unity, the Supreme Commander, who was responsible for every decision, could be certain that all the striking power of his vast resources in troops and supplies was available to take tactical advantage of opportunities offered us by the enemy's weakness and his mistakes in the field. Controlling all Allied military power, he could allocate it to any front for a decisive blow.

Without intending a full-dress appraisal of German leadership, it is certainly true that Hitler turned out to be his generals' own worst enemy. His "intuition," while strikingly successful for a time in the early years, was no substitute for the professional competence required to fight an equal and in the end a superior adversary. His strategy constantly proved that he was unable, after the two-front war began, to estimate soundly what his remaining resources in men and equipment would permit him to hold. Insisting fanatically, in faithful imitation of world "conquerors," on preserving all his conquests, in the end he lost everything.

The German generals, too, must take their share of the blame. They were overconfident behind their Atlantic Wall. They were particularly faulty in estimating the speed of our build-up on shore. Kesselring and Jodl told us they expected a landing of four divisions. They believed it would take five or six days to get these forces ashore. The fact was, our initial assault on the beaches was made with five divisions, plus two in the immediate follow-up. Seven divisions were ashore within twenty-four hours of the time the first waves went in. This great power threw the Germans off balance at the outset. Forced to rush troops to plug their line, they were unable to marshal forces for the strong counterattack which was the only weapon we had to fear in the days which followed the Normandy landings.

One salient fact emerges from any estimate of our victory. We had air superiority throughout the war. From D-Day onward, the German Air Force was never a major factor in the tactical battle. The Allies understood how to create and apply air power. The Germans, overconfident after their success in 1939 and 1940, neglected to improve and expand. The German Army obtained better weapons and for a time, at least, was able to fight a two-front war. This the Luftwaffe was never able to do. The development of land-air technique in the Allied forces to the point that every great battle was conceived and conducted as a combined affair—on some days more than twelve thousand sorties were flown in support of the ground forces—was one of the outstanding characteristics of the European campaign. Moreover, this doctrine came to be observed in a strategic as well as a tactical sense.

After his capture, Field Marshal von Rundstedt completely identified the Germans' failure with the downfall of the German Air Force. When it was suggested to him that the indications were the Allies were the superior fighters, he retorted: "Allied air superiority shattered our supply lines and upset all efforts to move our defense forces."

Although Rundstedt's belief was by no means the whole story of the German defeat, we had no quarrel with what he said. That was the way we planned it.

Epilogue to Victory

ELEVEN years have passed since that early morning
hour in the schoolhouse at Reims when General
Jodl signed his name to the document of surrender of
the military power of Germany. The time was 0241;
the date May 7, 1945. Hitler was dead, a suicide in his
Berlin bunker; everywhere the Nazi armies were in
flight. The Red armies were streaming west and our own
Allied forces had pushed two hundred miles to the east
of Berlin and south into the Bavarian Alps, where we
had feared a last bitter stand might be made. But it was
all over now.

The strange thing, as I think of it with the years between, was the lack of emotion that was shown when
the surrender was signed. The Germans—Jodl and Admiral von Friedeburg—were militarily correct in their
stonelike expressions. But I do not remember that any of
the Allied officers around the table displayed elation at
this ending of the long years of fighting. It was a moment
of solemn gratitude. When the signatures were all af-
fixed, we took the Germans briefly to see the Supreme

Commander. General Eisenhower had not wished to be present at the surrender and had assigned me the responsibility of representing him. But he wanted to say a brief, stern word to these representatives of the tyranny against which his great crusade was directed.

It was over quickly. He asked General Jodl if he understood thoroughly the meaning of the document he had signed, and told him he would be held officially and personally responsible if the terms of the surrender were violated. When Jodl replied that he understood, General Eisenhower said curtly, "That is all," and the interview was at an end.

Looking back over the eleven months of fighting which were required to defeat the German armies, I can say very sincerely that I do not believe a great campaign has ever been fought before with so little change in its original strategic plan. The grand strategy for OVERLORD which was agreed upon at SHAEF before the troops were ever put aboard ship for the invasion was followed almost without alteration. Tactical changes were made as the German reaction called for them, but the strategic plan was not changed.

As a matter of fact, only one really important variation in the tactical plan was made in the entire course of the European campaign. This was General Eisenhower's decision, described in the second of the six chapters, to abandon the operation to clear Brittany of the enemy and use the ports of the peninsula for the supply of American troops. This variation was dictated by two events: First, the remarkable success of the Third

Army in its sweep to the southeast and, second, the opportunity which the stubborn stand of the Germans in Normandy gave us to destroy their effective force in place. The climactic struggle in the Falaise pocket offered us the chance to cut the German Seventh Army to pieces (we were to meet it again, reformed, in the Ardennes), as well as Panzer Group West. With this accomplished, the facilities of the Brittany ports became much less important. Our eyes were on the Channel ports further east and nearer the areas where future battles would be fought.

In review, the major points of our strategic plan after our break-through to the Norman plains were these: 1) We expected to drive the enemy back in fairly good order to the prepared defenses of the Siegfried Line. Instead of this withdrawal to successive positions, the Germans chose to stand in Normandy till their power of resistance was broken. The Allied forces then drove east, and the need of the Brittany ports ended. 2) We intended to concentrate our power in the north for a crossing of the Rhine to strike at the Ruhr. This plan was followed at all times and carried through. 3) We intended to launch rapid and successive drives west of the Rhine to destroy great portions of the enemy's resisting forces. These operations were carried out. The German decision to stake everything on the desperate Ardennes counteroffensive—the Battle of the Bulge—actually worked to our ultimate advantage as it turned out. 4) We intended to take the Ruhr by classic double envelopment. This, too, was carried out. 5) We intended, having stilled Germany's industrial heart, to destroy the remainder of her armed forces wherever they might still exist. Reviewing the strategic plan now, I find no point where I really think it might have been improved in the light of subsequent knowledge. I believe it brought us victory in the shortest time we could have expected, since every part of it was directed at coming to grips with the German military power and destroying its fighting potential.

It is a tribute to the bravery of our fighting men and the skill of their tactical leaders that the Allied forces never suffered a real military defeat during the entire course of the European campaign. But it is also a monument to the efficiency of our services of supply and particularly to the superiority of our Air Force in destroying its opposition and disrupting the supply system of the enemy. At no time from the Normandy landings until the final defeat were the Germans able to take and hold the initiative. In fact, though they seized the initiative briefly in the Battle of the Bulge, costing us delay and losses, they never had more than a local advantage. Some time after the end of hostilities I looked over the headlines in the American newspapers during those December days. I realized then what a gloomy Christmas my country must have had. Reports of the situation in the press were so grave that it might have seemed the entire Allied cause was in danger. It was never in danger. General Eisenhower's timely decision to employ our general reserve to reinforce our defense in the Ardennes destroyed the possibility of German success. The story might have been somewhat different if our stubborn defense of Bastogne had been overwhelmed. But in the estimates of the situation when the offensive had been completely stopped it was apparent that the Germans could not have been successful in their ultimate objective, which was to seize Antwerp. Even though they had penetrated much further in their original thrust, even though they had crossed the Meuse, they would proceeded so far beyond their possibilities of supply that they could not have swept to the Channel. Theirs was a desperate undertaking, as the German generals recognized. It was foredoomed to failure, and with this failure all hope for German success in the West came to an end.

I have seen no reason to reappraise the actions and decisions of Supreme Headquarters in the Battle of the Ardennes or in the other campaigns which drew us up to the Rhine. The hazard of the Ardennes was considerably overestimated not only by our experienced correspondents but even by some of our Allies. The battle cost us time and heavy casualties, but it gave us an opportunity to inflict such critical losses on the enemy, in both men and matériel, that an effective German defense of the Siegfried Line and the Rhine became impossible.

One point which should be emphasized is that the objective of our planning was always to destroy the German power to make war. The liberation of friendly territory, or the capture of enemy territory, was incidental to the destruction of German military strength. Once this was accomplished, we should be free to move where we wished in Europe. That is why I said previously that the Battle of the Bulge actually was fought to our ultimate advantage. It is also the reason General Eisenhower rejected a proposal made in early September by Field Marshal Montgomery for a "knife-edge" attack on Berlin.

Following our swift progress across France and Belgium, the Field Marshal became convinced that if all supply were directed to his 21st Army Group, he could drive forward on a relatively narrow front with an attack which would carry him all the way to Berlin. He was sure that our offensive drive had demoralized the enemy forces. He now felt that the operation he proposed would cause the collapse of Germany and so end the war.

However attractive this prospect appeared, the condition of our overextended supply lines seemed to us to make it impossible to maintain sufficient forces for a drive of this kind deep into Germany. Nor would Montgomery have had a sufficient organization in the slender thrust he described to meet the certain and heavy reaction which the Germans could have directed against both flanks of his advance. This opinion was shared by several of the Field Marshal's senior staff officers, including his very able Chief of Staff, General de Guingand. As I hope these chapters have made clear, bravery of troops alone is not enough for victory in modern war. There must be the certainty of supply, as well as the necessary forces to protect flanks and keep the enemy from massing sufficient troops at any point to cut off the spearhead of the advance. The occupation of conquered territory is itself a great drain on the strength of an attacking army.

Even had the success of the Field Marshal's proposed operation seemed more probable, to concentrate all our supply and transport for his support would have completely halted operations on every other part of the front. This would not have been important if Montgomery's victory was rapid and complete. In any other alternative our other armies would have been almost immobilized through lack of both supply and transport. Thus they would have been unable to furnish reinforcements if the Berlin drive found itself in trouble.

The same would have been true if all supply had been given to any other part of the line. I believe there was disappointment in this country when General Patton's Third Army was halted that September because his rapidly advancing columns had outrun their supply lines. If our advance had been less swift, so that supply could have paced it, he could have penetrated further. But even if his narrow thrust had not been stopped by German concentration, it would have brought him to an area where it would have been practically impossible to supply him across the Rhine. Thus, at worst, we would have risked a serious military defeat.

But though General Eisenhower did not agree with Montgomery's plan to attempt a thin thrust to Berlin in early September, he wanted a line to the northeast to protect the port of Antwerp, and he felt that at the same time it might be possible to gain a bridgehead over the

Lower Rhine in Holland. Field Marshal Montgomery was eager to attempt this operation, which went by the code name of MARKET-GARDEN. Its most spectacular aspect was the employment of the newly formed First Allied Airborne Army, commanded by Lt. Gen. Lewis H. Brereton, in a drop over the Netherlands. If successful, the operation would turn the Germans' northern flank and greatly facilitate our later crossing in strength to encircle the Ruhr. As it turned out, this was the single operation of the entire European campaign which failed to succeed fully in holding an objective it had gained.

The drop took place on Sunday, September 17, in daylight. The troops engaged were the British 1st Airborne Division and the American XVIII Corps, composed of the 82nd and 101st Airborne divisions commanded by General Ridgeway. The Americans were to drop at Nijmegen and Eindhoven to capture the bridges over the Waal and Maas rivers, the British further north at Arnhem. In this case, the British 1st Airborne Division formed the spearhead. They would be deep in enemy territory, with the mission of seizing the bridges over the Lower Rhine.

This airborne operation was linked to a ground operation by the British Second Army. The Field Marshal's plan was to put down a "carpet" of airborne troops in front of the advancing ground force which would consolidate with its added strength the positions the paratroopers had occupied. The ground troops were then to move up to the Zuider Zee and cut the exit of German troops from Holland. There was no great difficulty in the American sectors, where opposition was relatively light. But there was serious trouble in the drop zone of the British 1st Airborne at Arnhem. These gallant troops encountered very strong opposition.

This was not entirely unexpected at SHAEF. Not long before the drop. Maj. Gen. Kenneth Strong, SHAEF G-2, came to me and expressed his belief that the area near the drop zone of the British division was occupied by several reduced-strength German armored divisions, possibly as many as four, which had been withdrawn from the line for refitting. General Strong had no real evidence of this. He knew these divisions had been withdrawn; he knew they must be somewhere in Holland. By a process of elimination, and with that sixth sense that sometimes comes to experienced Intelligence officers, he believed they were in the area around Arnhem. It was chiefly a matter of the vacuum of radio silence, he explained, when he told me of his fears. He had no proof, he repeated, that the German armored divisions were in the Arnhem area. But if they weren't there, where were they?

I took him in to see the Supreme Commander. If General Strong was right, the 1st Airborne Division could not hold out against the power the Germans could bring to bear against it, and the ground troops would have difficulty reaching the area, too. Granted the German divisions were severely attenuated, there could still be four of them; and, if so, no single division could hold out against the firepower they could mass.

General Eisenhower considered the situation with the

greatest care. He said quite rightly that since General Strong had no real evidence or identification to support his belief, he could not order Field Marshal Montgomery, who was in tactical command of the operation, to change his plan. But he told us to take a plane immediately, go to Montgomery's headquarters, and tell him of the suspected position of the German divisions. The Field Marshal would then have to decide whether Strong's unconfirmed conclusion was more plausible than the estimate of his own Intelligence.

We followed the Supreme Commander's order, and we gave the Field Marshal our own recommendation that to ensure the safety of the operation he should drop two airborne divisions in the Arnhem area instead of one. Montgomery rejected our suggestion, and the operation proceeded according to plan. General Strong had been right about the German armor. It was in the area of Arnhem. Though the British 1st Airborne Division fought skillfully and heroically, the men could not hold out against such a superiority of enemy troops. By September 25 the remnants of the gallant division were withdrawn, without having accomplished the mission of crossing the Lower Rhine. On the other hand, the foothold we had gained further south in Holland was of incalculable benefit in securing our possession of the great port of Antwerp. Following the airborne operation, attacks by the British and Canadians succeeded in clearing the approaches to Antwerp by defeating the Germans on Walcheren Island and in South Beveland. Though we had not crossed the Rhine, we had opened

Antwerp, a great avenue of supply which was to serve us till the end of the campaign.

On September 1, General Eisenhower had taken tactical command of all ground forces in the battle zone. This arrangement was always part of the strategic plan. Field Marshal Montgomery was to have tactical command of ground troops until we were firmly established on the Continent and the American 12th Army Group was in being, at which time General Eisenhower would assume tactical command. In late August, the Field Marshal proposed that he continue to exercise tactical control of all ground forces in addition to commanding the 21st Army Group. In practical fact, this would have meant that General Eisenhower was abandoning his authority as Supreme Commander, for it was his responsibility to exercise general tactical control over the huge area of the entire front. With the needs and assigned missions of the various forces familiar to him, he alone could have the knowledge to allocate supplies and divisions for the separate operations. Had Montgomery, too, been in a position to reassign units and allocate supplies for forces other than his own, serious confusion could have resulted. General Eisenhower rightly refused to consider the Field Marshal's proposal as workable.

But from time to time, and particularly after the Battle of the Bulge had necessitated giving Montgomery temporary control of the American First and Ninth armies, this conception was revived, though usually only in the British press. It was always vigorously resisted by General Eisenhower as incompatible with his responsibility as Supreme Commander, and his position was supported by the Combined Chiefs of Staff. The command setup remained throughout the war as it had been originally planned.

General Eisenhower exercised active command of the European front. The high-level meetings with heads of state and other dignitaries which were a necessity of his supreme headquarters never prevented him from close and active contact with the armies on every part of the front. He was constantly on the move, visiting his subordinate commanders and talking with their troops— the only way a commander can maintain the feel of the situation, and judge the morale of officers and men, and their combat capabilities.

He was, and always considered himself, strictly a military commander, in accordance with the Combined Chiefs of Staff's directive from which he obtained his authority. I make the point because I have occasionally heard the question raised as to why the Americans did not rush for Berlin and seize it before the Russians could take the German capital. The reason, as has been pointed out in an earlier chapter, was solely military. Our mission was to destroy the power of Germany to continue the war. This meant finding, engaging, and destroying enemy armies wherever they could be encountered. We were gravely concerned, following the capture of the Ruhr, that the remaining German forces should not be allowed a chance to regroup and meet us again. We were also concerned with the reports, too frequent to be disregarded, that the Nazis intended to seek the mountain fastness of the Bavarian Alps and make a last-ditch resistance fight to the finish.

From the military point of view, to have diverted a force large enough to take Berlin would have been unjustified. Berlin had become a geographical objective only, and the Russians were already converging on the city in force. Its fall was only a matter of days.

For some years there seemed to be, and possibly there still remains, some misapprehension that, had we taken Berlin ahead of the Russians, we would have remained in possession of it, and so forestalled some of the difficulties we were later to encounter with the Soviet occupation. If this exists, it is due to lack of recognition of the reality of the political arrangements which had already been decided by the heads of state for the occupation zones of the various Allied nations. By tripartite agreement, undertaken before we crossed the Channel, the American and British zones of occupation were placed two hundred miles to the west of Berlin.

The division of Berlin itself, as an enclave with Russian, British, and American compartments had been decided on at the same time (later a French zone was also delimited). In the atmosphere of friendliness which was supposed to exist at that period between the Eastern and Western cobelligerents, the violation on our part of an agreement already reached would have been interpreted by our own people, as well as by the Russians, as gross ill faith. In the ensuing outcry, I personally feel sure we could not have stood our ground.

Prime Minister Churchill expressed his contrary view

to me when we were lunching alone in London shortly after the cessation of hostilities but before any arrangements had been made with the Russians. He believed our forces should remain for the time being where they were, deep in the Soviet zone. He felt it was a grave mistake for the American and British troops, as he put it, to withdraw from this area which they had won by their blood, lives, and courage before definite agreements on various aspects of the occupation were reached with the Soviet Union.

I disagreed at the time, not with the theory but with the practicality. I felt public opinion was too strong in both our countries. I reminded him that for several years both the British and American people had been led to believe by our information agencies that the Soviet Union was our most important and valuable cobelligerent and that the possibility for continued mutual understanding in the future was good. It would, I thought, be almost impossible for us to keep troops in the Soviet Zone over the Russians' protest.

Mr. Churchill more accurately estimated our future relationships with the Soviet Union than any Western statesman who dealt with them. It was impossible for most of us at that time to realize the lengths to which distrust could carry the Russians in their dealing with the West.

It is true that in the field we had one remarkable demonstration of their suspicion. In those last days of the war the Germans were desperately attempting to surrender to the Western rather than the Eastern powers.

In fact, at the surrender talks in Reims, first Admiral von Friedeburg and then General Jodl attempted to delay the proceedings with, I am sure, the purpose of permitting as many as possible of the German troops and civilians to escape into the arms of the West.

But the Russians apparently believed—for what reason I do not know but now can estimate—that we intended to make a separate peace with the Germans and even to accept these Nazi enemies as our allies for a counteroffensive against the Soviet. Along the Russian front during that last week of hostilities loudspeakers were constantly blaring at the Germans. "You are about to be made the victims of the greatest treachery in history," their message ran. "If you surrender to the Americans or British, they intend to force you to turn your guns against your Russian comrades!" In the light of their past experience with the Russians, it seems doubtful that this propaganda had its effect on the harried Germans. They continued to make every effort to be captured by us. But it is possible the Russians had convinced themselves that what they were broadcasting was true since, had they been in our position, it is probably what they would have done themselves.

Only lack of direct contact, the necessity of a certain amount of propaganda in favor of a cobelligerent in war, and, of course, a certain amount of wishful thinking, would have impelled any objective and intelligent person to arrive at the conclusion that when the war was over the attitude of the Soviet Government would really be friendly. General Deane, the head of our military mission in Moscow, reported that his experience was one frustration after another. The Russians would always give the absolute minimum to get what they were determined to have. In the beginning, most of us knew little about Russia. We had no way of knowing. But from what we did learn—in North Africa and later—there was enough to justify serious apprehensions. Those of us who encountered them earlier reached these pessimistic conclusions earlier, and many were criticized for so doing. But while there was an occasional officer like Marshal Zhukov who seemed, at least, to appreciate the importance of frank dealing and an East-West understanding, other commanders, and particularly their political officers, were very different.

General Eisenhower's directive as Supreme Commander reserved contact with the Russians to the Combined Chiefs of Staff. And until we were approaching what were obviously to be the final battles of the war, we had no direct contact with them. When it was apparent that our eastward-probing spearheads must presently meet the Russians, General Eisenhower asked for and received permission to send a military delegation to Moscow. He designated his deputy, Air Chief Marshal Tedder, to head this group. Until he returned we felt real concern over what might happen when an American or British force encountered the Russians. Even so simple a matter as informing each other of the conventional markings of our planes and vehicles, so that they could be recognized by both sides from air or ground, had never been undertaken. Through the press and in official pronouncements the public was given to understand that there was a closeness between the Western and Eastern opponents of Germany. Actually, there was no understanding between the two nations in the field. We had only the most general knowledge of the whereabouts and battle intentions of the Soviet forces. What we feared most was an encounter between armored elements and that, through lack of recognition, a fire fight might take place that could have the most serious implications.

As it turned out, when American and Soviet units met at the Elbe, they recognized each other, and relations between the two forces were for the time being completely cordial. Nevertheless, in more ways than one, it would be accurate to say that we did not speak the same language. We were now at the point where the friendship between the Eastern and Western Allies, of which the American and British peoples had been convinced, was to be demonstrated as fact or fiction. At SHAEF it gradually became very clear that there was no real basis of alliance, except in name. Soviet officials grew increasingly aloof, suspicious, and intransigent. That this was simply high-echelon Soviet policy is evidenced by the friendliness between individual members of the Red Army and our own troops during their contact in the field. Later the Soviet Government corrected these "errors," and all ranks of the Red Army confined their contacts with our troops to official or formal necessities.

In the years since 1945 I have had more experience with the Communist government of the Soviet Union.

For three years, while Ambassador in Moscow, I experienced the frustrations of that embassy while stating the American position to Stalin and others in authority. But as long ago as our North African days I had had my introduction to Soviet methods. This began when the Mediterranean Commission was formed to consider the future government of Italy when we should have secured the surrender of the Fascist dictatorship. Mr. Andrei Vishinsky headed the Soviet delegation, and we soon realized the scorn of the Russians for the unimportance (to them) of this little "side-show" military operation we were conducting from North Africa. On the other hand, the great importance they attached to the political future of Italy became equally apparent. Mr. Vishinsky immediately demanded that the Russian officers be given an opportunity to visit the Allied front in Italy. We knew that Allied officers in Moscow had frequently requested permission to visit the Russian front and that these requests had been ignored or refused. However, it seemed to me that a useful purpose might be served in having the Russians visit the Allied front, which was just then before Monte Cassino, and we acceded to Vishinsky's demand. I asked Gen. Francis W. de Guinguand, Field Marshal Montgomery's Chief of Staff, to make sure the Russians saw some action.

The Soviet officers returned somewhat impressed by their experience. One of them said to me, "I can die for Mother Russia—in Russia—any time. I don't have to come to Italy to do it." Aside from the basic and deep-rooted antagonism of the Soviet political system to our own, there was no reason whatever why the Soviet Government should have denied Allied officers such visits. They had nothing to be ashamed of. Whatever we may think of the Kremlin, the courage and fortitude of the Red Army during the war were outstanding.

I had few contacts with the Russians in North Africa. There were no Soviet troops there, and the presence of a delegation was political rather than military. Similarly, through the planning for the OVERLORD operation and the European campaign, there was no military contact until the very end. I think in this country the impression existed that there was friendly collaboration between the two military commands. This is not correct. The Combined Chiefs of Staff had no intimate contact to pass on to General Eisenhower. We worked along as distant associates against a common enemy until the necessity finally arrived of meeting and recognizing each other. We know now that there was no closeness at any level in the contact with Moscow. Only, on the side of the Kremlin, deep suspicion.

After the cessation of hostilities, when we moved to our new occupation headquarters in Frankfurt, we began to feel the first pinpricks, then the aggressiveness of the Soviet command in trying our determination, which later reached its climax in the Berlin blockade.

But Russian intransigence and the difficulty of dealing with men of ill will are not what I like to remember of the European campaign. It is far more satisfying, and more encouraging for the future, to recall instead the friendship, the dedication, and the determination of the

Index

Aachen, capture of, 87
Air attacks: to isolate northwest France, 23, 37–38; retaliation in Ardennes, 105; in the Ruhr, 163–64
Allied airborne units
  See American XVIII Corps, American 17th Airborne Division, American 82nd Airborne Division, American 101st Airborne Division, British 1st Airborne Division, British 6th Airborne Division, First Allied Airborne Army
American Army groups:
  6TH ARMY GROUP (American Seventh Army and French First Army): advances toward Schweinfurth, Stuttgart, and Nürnberg, 195; in Berchtesgaden, 201; captures Colmar, 125; containing Colmar pocket, 90; drives through High Vosges in Belfort Gap area, 87; end of resistance toward, in southern zone, 125; American division added to French army, 125; in Hagenau, 144; links with American Third Army, 57, with American

Fifth Army, 178; in Munich, 195; in southern France, 84
12TH ARMY GROUP: *American First Army*: in Ardennes, 104, 106; attacks toward Cologne, 128, 137; breaches Siegfried Line, 87; captures Cherbourg, 74; commanded by Bradley, 4, 118, by Hodges, 58, by Montgomery, 104; composed of two corps for invasion, 12; divisions of: 1st, in Ardennes, 104, 2nd, in Ardennes, 104, 4th, in Ardennes, 104, 7th Armored, in Ardennes, 93, 9th Armored, in Ardennes, 92, 104, takes Remagen, 139–140, 28th in Ardennes, 91, 60th, in Brittany ports, 149, 69th, meets Russians at Elbe, 196, 99th, in Ardennes, 104, 106th, in Ardennes, 91, 104; erupts from Remagen bridgehead, 160; in Frankfort corridor north to Kassel, 160; at Harz Mountains, 190, 191; headquarters at Bristol, 11; joins with American Third Army at Houffalize, 106; with Russians at Torgau, 196; in Normandy break-through, 77;

231